Rolling Stone

Images of Rock & Roll

Rolling Stone
Images *of* Rock & Roll

———————

Edited and Designed by

Fred Woodward

———————

Text by

Anthony DeCurtis

Little, Brown and Company

BOSTON　　NEW YORK　　TORONTO　　LONDON

A Rolling Stone Press Book

EDITOR Holly George-Warren
ASSOCIATE EDITOR Shawn Dahl
EDITORIAL ASSISTANT Greg Emmanuel
DESIGNER Fred Woodward
PHOTO EDITORS Denise Sfraga, Julie Claire Derscheid
DESIGN ASSOCIATE Fredrik Sundwall
DESIGN ASSISTANTS Yoomi Chong, Su-Mei Chan
PRODUCTION EDITOR Eric Flaum
EDITORIAL CONTRIBUTORS Anthony DeCurtis,
    Susan Richardson, Nancy Bilyeau, Will Rigby
TYPOGRAPHER Eric Siry

First Edition

ISBN 0-316-75468-4

Library of Congress Catalog
Card Number 95-76662

10 9 8 7 6 5 4 3 2 1

IM

Published simultaneously in Canada
by Little, Brown & Company (Canada)
Limited

Printed in Hong Kong

The Goudy Type used in this book was
    rendered digitally by Richard Beatty.

Dion © Alfred Wertheimer, all rights reserved
Bob Dylan and Joan Baez © 1967 Daniel Kramer
Janis Joplin © Bob Seidemann
Iggy Pop by Robert Mapplethorpe © 1981 The Estate
    of Robert Mapplethorpe
Prince by Terry Gydesen originally appeared in
    The Sacrifice of Victor © 1994 Paisley Park Enterprises
Bonnie Raitt © Bill King, 1975/Bill King Photographs, Inc.
Patti Smith by Bill King © Bill King, 1976/Bill King
    Photographs, Inc.
Patti Smith by Robert Mapplethorpe © 1978 The Estate
    of Robert Mapplethorpe
Ike and Tina Turner © 1995 Dennis Hopper
Village People © Bill King, 1979/Bill King Photographs, Inc.

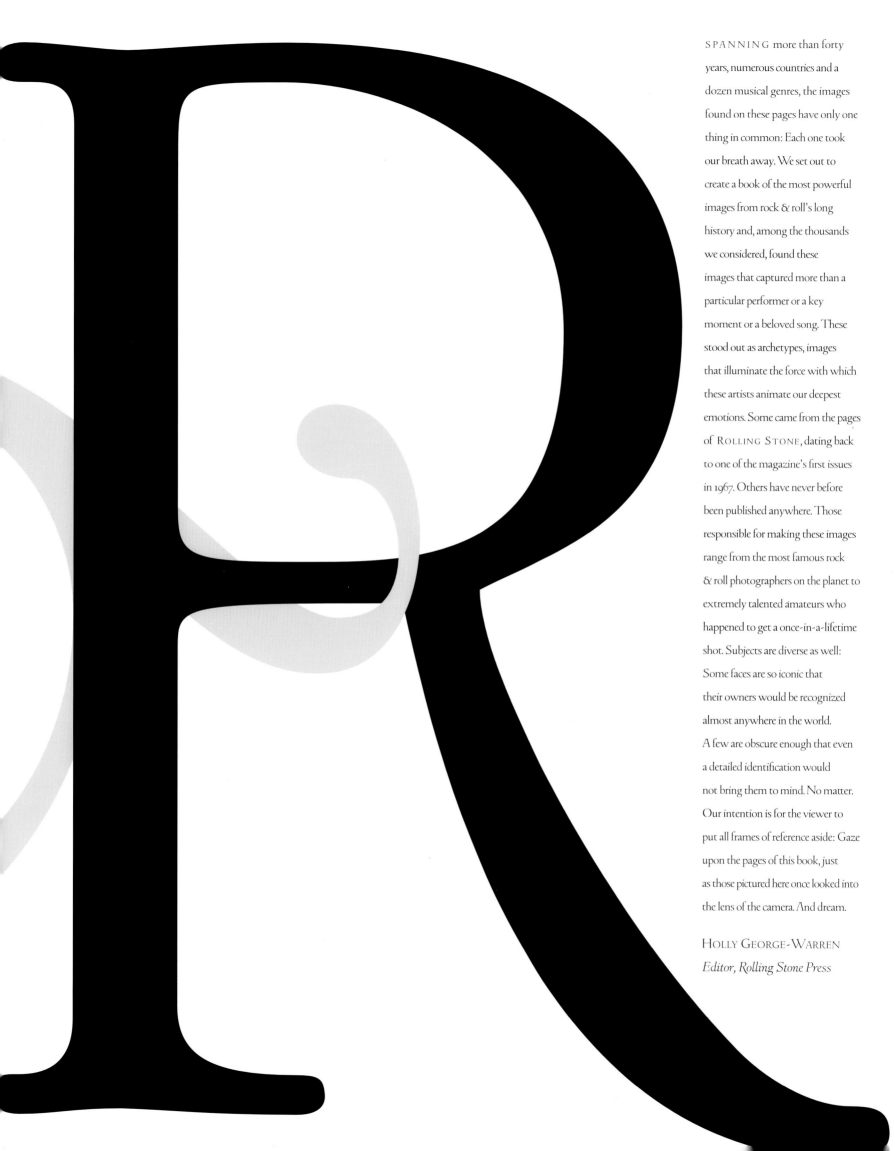

SPANNING more than forty years, numerous countries and a dozen musical genres, the images found on these pages have only one thing in common: Each one took our breath away. We set out to create a book of the most powerful images from rock & roll's long history and, among the thousands we considered, found these images that captured more than a particular performer or a key moment or a beloved song. These stood out as archetypes, images that illuminate the force with which these artists animate our deepest emotions. Some came from the pages of ROLLING STONE, dating back to one of the magazine's first issues in 1967. Others have never before been published anywhere. Those responsible for making these images range from the most famous rock & roll photographers on the planet to extremely talented amateurs who happened to get a once-in-a-lifetime shot. Subjects are diverse as well: Some faces are so iconic that their owners would be recognized almost anywhere in the world. A few are obscure enough that even a detailed identification would not bring them to mind. No matter. Our intention is for the viewer to put all frames of reference aside: Gaze upon the pages of this book, just as those pictured here once looked into the lens of the camera. And dream.

HOLLY GEORGE-WARREN
Editor, Rolling Stone Press

THE "LOOK," the visual creation and expression of an identity, is part of the very essence of rock & roll. But the relationship between the look and the sound has always been tense. After all, what could the art of photography – with its connotations of high-gloss fashion shoots, tony museum culture and the studied concentration of studio portraiture – really have to do with rock & roll, the sweat-soaked music of the moment, most at home in clubs and juke joints, most powerful when it's most visceral? We must first of all remember that even the grittiest performance is visual to a profound extent. Our everyday language itself reveals that: We are far more likely to say that we went to "see" a band than hear one. The look is certainly not more significant than the music, not in any lasting sense. But no music is entirely pure; no music is exclusively about itself, exclusively about sound. The look can very legitimately be said to be part of our experience of the music. David Bowie and Jackson Browne, Snoop Doggy Dogg and Paul McCartney, Carly Simon and Courtney Love: We would hear their music differently if they presented themselves to us visually in different ways. More important, though, as with every other significant art form, rock & roll's truest, most compelling force lies not in reckless abandon, not in anarchy, but in the taut, dynamic interplay between abandon and control. If we were not already intimately familiar with the beautiful, still features of the young Elvis Presley or Pearl Jam's Eddie Vedder, for example, performance shots of those artists would have no emotional context and therefore no real meaning. So the look and the music are inevitably married, subverting and reinforcing, stating the obvious and exploring the unknown, documenting and transforming, till death do them part. ON A SIMPLER LEVEL, photographers have access to times and places in the lives of artists that we do not, and it's a kick to sneak inside with them. How touching it is to see Aretha Franklin, a singer of monumental talent but a notoriously awkward performer, standing shyly, her eyes averted, in a New York studio with choreographer Cholly Atkins in 1961, years before she would be recognized as one of the giants of soul music. The possessor of a great vocal gift that she would later give to the world, she is trying to learn a physical language, a way of being Aretha Franklin as the eyes of others look on. And what a delight to see the incomparable Dion DiMucci, the cocky doo-wop bard of the Bronx, sitting down for a meal with his mom, who, from her facial expression, takes her cooking seriously. This shot reminds us that photos can recall images from other media, from other times and places. One look at Dion's carefully coiffed hair inevitably brings to mind John Travolta under siege from his family at the dinner table in *Saturday Night Fever*, a hand and a hairdo across generations, style as a visual rebellion. SOMETIMES IT MAY TAKE a while to get them to agree, but when artists consent to do photo shoots, it's as if they've decided to come out and play, to explore new sides of themselves, to wander out beyond the edges of the identity their fans may be most familiar with, to shed one look for another. Or sometimes they just plunge deeper into an identity they have already crafted. With photographer Henry Diltz in 1972, the Eagles plundered history to craft an image appropriate to the feel of the American West that informs their music. In a shoot for their second album, *Desperado*, they cast themselves (and their friends Jackson Browne and J.D. Souther) as slain outlaws displayed on the ground as trophies by the lawmen who brought them low. That was how the West was won – the historical photo was clearly meant to demonstrate that lawlessness would not prevail, that rule of law would rule the frontier. But Diltz and the Eagles understood that in the fractious America of the early seventies, viewers (whose sensibility was partly shaped by movies like *Bonnie and Clyde* and songs like Woody Guthrie's "Pretty Boy Floyd," works of art about heroic criminals in rebellion against a corrupt system) would sympathize with the beautiful, glamorous losers. "To live outside the law you must be honest," sang Bob Dylan, the inheritor of Guthrie's mantle, in the sixties – from traditional folk music to contemporary gangster rap, imagery that defines artists as beyond confining social codes adds to their allure, the romance of their outsider status. WHEN THE ARTIST and the photographer enjoy a friendship based on mutual trust, the willingness to experiment can produce especially telling results. Anyone who believes Bono to be ascetic and overly serious might have second thoughts after seeing Anton Corbijn's 1993 portrait of him in a posh New York hotel taking a bubble bath, complete with a glass of champagne and his Fly shades, a justifiably worried George Bush – the man who thought Boy George was in U2 – peering over his shoulder. In all likelihood, only Corbijn, who has worked with U2 for many years, could have gotten Bono to fool around so freely. And would the notoriously private Bob Dylan have consented to bounce on a trampoline or pose with his son Jesse (now a photographer himself) for a photographer he knew less well than Elliott Landy? Historical context provides drama to such photographs, a drama hidden from viewers decades down the line. The initial shock of those photographs was seeing the spokesman for a generation, the voice at the barricades, in repose, in retreat, even having fun. The bard of protest turns out to be a family man. The paradox is that once an artist permits a photographer into his personal life the secret world becomes known, revelation yields to the ordinariness of everyday life, and the look of domesticity becomes as much a part of the artist's iconography as the most hyped publicity shot. Then the identity as a private person and a recluse is the identity that must be escaped. ALLOWED TO MINGLE with one another, freed from the constraints of chronology and history, liberated from ego and artistic concerns, photographs can strike up conversations with each other, create fields of emotional energy between themselves. Both character and style can speak. Jimi Hendrix and Bob Marley never met in their lives; they left this world too early. But as Hendrix sang, "If I don't see you no more in this world/I'll meet you in the next one, and don't be late." Now Hendrix and Marley meet in the symbolic afterworld of images. In his 1967 portrait, Gered Mankowitz presents Hendrix as a black Sgt. Pepper, a spellbinding blend of physical grace and outrageousness, invitation and confrontation. While Hendrix coolly smokes a cigarette, Marley blows a sacramental spliff. In Dennis Morris's photo, Marley himself seems on fire, burning with righteousness, his eyes shut in ecstasy, the smoke around him emerging from an inner flame. If Hendrix is a hipper Sgt. Pepper, a Pied Piper to the burgeoning Woodstock Nation, Marley is Natty Dread, the folkloric embodiment of an oppressed people's will to rise up and seize freedom, to catch a fire and spread it. American and Jamaican, Hendrix and Marley are black brothers, their beautiful, slender fingers pointing the way to political liberation and spiritual transcendence. The great blues master Muddy Waters, elegant and dignified in a suit, exudes the calm, concentrated power of a Buddha as he strums a guitar in a darkened dressing room. Meanwhile, Elvis Presley – the conduit through whom black vernacular music would travel to main-street America – stops to sign an autograph for some fans. If Muddy Waters is the embodiment of a kind of ancient, elemental wisdom, his adopted name an evocation of the great and mighty Mississippi River, Presley, his bicycle resting between his legs, is the teenager as celebrity, the new icon, delivered by the postwar prosperity of the American fifties, that would reshape the world. "The blues had a baby and they named it rock & roll," Waters wrote, and these two pictures tell that story of a father and his bastard son. A grieving Yoko Ono, photographed by Annie Leibovitz for the first time after John Lennon's death, is haunted by the proximity of the young Lennon she never knew, a memory after the fact, as well as by her knowledge of the grown man, her husband and lover, whom she saw murdered and whom she will never again see in this world. Lennon, for his part, seems presciently stoic and sad in Astrid Kirchherr's shadowy black and white portrait of him, from 1962. He was "an immense personality that had already known much pain," Kirchherr says, the bearer of "wisdom beyond his years." Lennon's friend Stu Sutcliffe had recently died; Lennon's mother was the earlier primal loss that would define all losses for him. In his own death he would be taken away from Yoko, the mother-lover who had restored all that had been taken away from him. INTERACTIONS AMONG IMAGES can sometimes get edgy. Bluesman Lightnin' Hopkins, a true master of the Texas-radio big beat that inspired Jim Morrison, stands in tense relation to the Lizard King. For Morrison, a watermelon is the stuff of sensuality and fertility rites, a ripe offering from a young god to photographer Alan Ronay and, through Ronay, to the Doors' Dionysian followers. The visual presence of Hopkins, whose personal force and hard experience carry him out of the frame of Jean Pierre LeLoir's portrait and into Morrison's world, makes us uncomfortable about accepting Morrison's gift, however innocently offered. The world outside the photograph inevitably shapes how a photograph will be viewed, how it can be viewed. Race is an issue that cannot be escaped. Jim Morrison can be photographed holding a watermelon, but Lightnin' Hopkins cannot. Were the blues stolen and exploited, or exposed to a larger audience by worshipful acolytes? What is the meaning of a piece of fruit? It depends on who is offering it and who is looking on. And why is Snoop Doggy Dogg, born Calvin Broadus in California, looking suspiciously and sidelong at Mississippi Fred McDowell over a gulf of twenty-four years? Could it be the complex relationship between young, urban African-Americans and their ancestors' rural past? The contemporaneity and purgative violence of rap and the age-old timelessness, suffering and spiritual triumph of the blues? Whatever it may be – neither of these men, each powerful and proud, is giving any quarter. Similarly, L.L. Cool J's raw physicality in Albert Watson's portrait of him takes on an unsettling aspect under the calm gaze of Curtis Mayfield, who was photographed by Mark Seliger in 1994. Mayfield, who is paralyzed from the neck down as the result of an accident, seems possessed of a metaphysical understanding, a kind of nobility born of his affliction and his bearing of it. His look is accepting and benign, as if to say to his younger brother: "You are youthful and strong, but there are things you do not know yet. You will learn them eventually." Sometimes the conversation suggested by an image is really a monologue, a riveting soliloquy. What, really, is there to say when confronted by David Gahr's thrilling 1966 photo of the magnificent Howlin' Wolf ripping up the stage? Do you really want to interrupt this man, let him know what's on your mind, share your point of view? Leaning urgently forward, roaring into a microphone that he seems to be crushing with his left hand, pointing at the crowd, Wolf appears under the impression that he has something to say. Best stay out of the way and let him say it. The photograph succeeds in precisely the opposite way from the performance itself. Held still in two dimensions, Wolf is eternally in motion. Wolf's energy is so strong, so unstoppable, he seems about to haul his entire band off the stage, through the photographic frame, and on through the rest of this book. CLOTHES AND PROPS and makeup and faces can tell stories – one look at Raeanne Rubenstein's picture of Peter Gabriel transforming himself before going onstage demonstrates that. Does Gabriel view himself as a warrior preparing to enter battle or a clown whose purpose is to entertain a jaded public? Rock stars are a bit of both, and their performances both pander and assault, flatter and challenge. So embellishing the body is a way of telling stories. But what are the stories the body itself can tell to a camera? Sometimes a willingness to expose the body in nature communicates not wantonness but openness and innocence, as it does in Laura Levine's portrait of a nude Björk frolicking in the woods, catching raindrops on her tongue: "And they were both naked, the man and his wife, and were not ashamed." It is the body free of adornments and affectations, ignorant of shame, the unaccommodated woman, the unaccommodated man. The Allman Brothers' readiness to strip down for photographer Stephen Paley tells us that these musicians are bonded like a family, that they are brothers, if not all by blood, then in their souls. They are comfortable being totally exposed to one another (like soldiers, or a sports team in the locker room or shower) as well as to the photographer and, ultimately, the viewer. If you know that the Allman Brothers are a Southern band, there is an additional, larger message: The presence of a black man, drummer Jai Johanny Johanson, in this paradisiacal brotherhood suggests that a new day has dawned in a previously blighted land. Set in a cool stream in unspoiled woods, the photo tells us that the agrarian-utopian dreams of the sixties – getting back to the land and living a communal life – have found a fertile home in the rock & roll of the rural South. It is a prelapsarian world, before clothes were needed or even thought to be needed, before the tribes separated and scattered to the ends of the earth. The nude body can also be a sign that someone is in peril, at risk, a target – remember the naked fat man in the crowd at Altamont? In Bob Seidemann's affecting nude portraits of her, Janis Joplin is an exile from Eden, an injured angel, a being thoroughly, fleshily human but defenseless, all too exposed to the world and its dangers. In paradise, she would have been safe, but she is not safe here, not safe now. Sinéad O'Connor seems similarly vulnerable in Albert Watson's striking portrait of her, huddled under the wings of an angel for protection like a frightened Dickensian child. As with Joplin, O'Connor has shed her feistiness and her contentiousness with her clothes, revealing the girl inside the woman, the child inside the adult. It's hard to imagine anyone seeming less vulnerable than the Red Hot Chili Peppers in Mark Seliger's 1992 portrait of the band. Opposite Joplin's softness and sadness, the Chili Peppers are indurate and combative, their nakedness an attack, a provocation, a fuck you. There is nothing demure about the placement of their hands over their genitals; in fact, it seems almost a lewd gesture. It is only the slightest concession to civility, more for your sake than theirs, though their clear assumption is that you're missing out. The photo is a sexual taunt – they could be concealing themselves or fondling themselves – and a demand: "Here we are like this. What are you going to do about it?" No less sexually charged and controversial a figure than the Chili Peppers, a shirtless Axl Rose seems surprisingly gentle, almost forlorn, his chaos finally quieted, "one of the most sensitive people I've ever photographed," according to Herb Ritts, who shot him in 1991. Rose's tattoos seem touchingly sentimental, emotional expressions he would have a hard time articulating any other way. OTHER BODIES HAVE other, more disturbing things to say. Literally bent over backward onstage in Claude Gassian's 1977 concert photograph, Iggy Pop states that he

must contort himself to convey convincingly the brutalities of his world – and our world. In his persona as "the Idiot," Iggy embodies the freak as prophet and moral messenger, the tormented outsider as the ravaged conscience of the culture. (That element of Iggy is also superbly captured in Robert Mapplethorpe's stark 1981 studio portrait, which depicts the punk pioneer as a modern-day Cassandra.) Anyone not bent out of shape by this world is damnably implicated in its evils. Set side by side, the naked torsos of Sid Vicious and Henry Rollins dramatize two contradictory visions of the ideology of punk. Each man's body is an explicitly written text, a manifesto. In Bob Gruen's concert shot from the Sex Pistols' 1978 tour, Vicious's face, chest and arms are a map of self-laceration, a paean to pain and self-destructive excess. This photo could serve to illustrate the Nirvana song "I Hate Myself and I Want to Die," a parodic title that eventually took on a merciless reality. On the other hand, for Henry Rollins, shot while engaged in a preshow ritual in Japan in 1994 by Julian Broad ("I have never photographed anyone who affected me as much as Henry," Broad said later), to be a punk is to be a samurai. The body, in his eyes, is simultaneously a temple, a machine and a weapon, your last line of defense against the pillages of society. Taking care of it is a holy process, as much a statement as your art, the flesh made word. Rollins's back is emblazoned with the title of a song by Iggy Pop (whose own body, as we know, has a story or two to tell, which is why he has never hesitated to display it): "Search and Destroy," at once a desolate cry from one of the forefathers of punk ("I'm the world's forgotten boy/The one who searches to destroy") and a military term for the missions American soldiers would execute in the effort to locate and exterminate the Viet Cong and their sympathizers in rural Vietnam. Rollins exploits both the artistic and military associations of the slogan written (significantly, not carved, as in Vicious's case) on his body, which has been honed to a hard, pure perfection. Rollins is both desperate and aggressive, aggressive because he is desperate. If the grueling physical routine he adopts to achieve that state is a kind of self-punishment, it is in the interest of self-discipline and spiritual mastery. It is an exaltation of his body. Society is soft and flabby, weak, barely worthy to be your enemy. You are like iron, in your thinking, in your muscles, in your will, in your music, in your look. MUSICIANS AND MOVEMENT: The road has been a time-honored theme throughout the history of rock & roll, the pilgrimage from town to town a combination of excitement and unbearable tedium, the road of excess and excessive boredom, the lost highway, a quest, a sexual adventure and a tiresome ordeal. The rush of performance is pitted against the dullness of the bus or the van and the anonymity of hotels, airports and train stations. The thrilling sense of imminent possibility at the heart of travel struggles against the absence of home. Adoring crowds alternate with excruciating isolation. Anton Corbijn's moody, grainy image of Peter Gabriel wandering the winding road near his home in Bath, England, exquisitely evokes the metaphor of the rock & roll journey, which, for Gabriel, is an inner journey as well, with a goal of self-realization. Next to that picture, David Gahr's stunning portrait in profile of Emmylou Harris – her gaze lifted upward, her neck and hair extending behind her in a graceful curve, like a road she has traveled – intimates belief that at the end of the journey lies deliverance, salvation. It is a woman's body as a landscape, informed by the hope that lifts sacred country music, a source of inspiration for Harris, the road of a musical life as a stairway to heaven. Art Kane's portrait of Cream (featuring an unlikely looking Eric Clapton on the left, whose visual image has shifted with startling regularity over the years, sporting a mustache and wearing a wool cap, shades and pink boots) depicts the band's three members seated on railroad tracks that extend into the horizon behind them. The location reflects the uneasy relationship among Clapton, drummer Ginger Baker and bassist Jack Bruce during Cream's short, tempestuous life – railroad tracks are hardly a place to relax and unwind. This is not the Allman Brothers communing in the woods. Cream is literally in harm's way. Michael Jackson, though, is sitting pretty in the pilot's seat in Barry Plummer's charming portrait, shot at London's Gatwick Airport in 1972. From the cockpit of the Jackson 5's private plane, Jackson leans out the window and cracks the huge, irresistible smile that won the hearts of millions when he was a boy. Years before his unprecedented and still unmatched triumphs (*Thriller* is a decade away) and the endless scandals and rumors that would chip away at his stature (among many other things, his innocent face at this time had not yet felt the surgeon's scalpel), Jackson exudes the energy, exuberance and good cheer that made him one of popular music's greatest and most lovable performers. His childlike joy at being in the cockpit of a plane and wearing the captain's hat is completely unaffected – and completely infectious. In Lewis Allen's photograph from the late fifties, Buddy Holly sinks into his seat and into his coat after being driven back onto a tour bus by a screaming crowd of young girls in Rochester, New York. What's happening outside the bus is nowhere reproduced in Holly's expression, which is serious and inward looking, a far cry from the optimism and delicate yearning of his songs. He's concentrating, thinking about tonight's show or the problems with last night's, a still center in the storm his renown has created. Or maybe he's simply tired, another quotidian reality of the road. ROCK & ROLL has been said to be about little more than cars and girls – another aspect of the lives of musicians in motion – but mobility and sex are far from its only subjects. True, the appeal of fast, fancy cars can't be denied when you look at the late, great Gene Vincent lighting up behind the wheel of a sports car, or at Dr. Dre blazing by photographer Mark Seliger. The case for the sybaritic pleasure of cars has been convincingly made time and time again – but it's not the only case. Even that ultimate symbol of self-indulgent rock & roll success, the limousine, is not always a luxurious pleasure-mobile. For Prince, a hermit of hedonism, his limousine is another necessary layer of insulation against the intrusions of the external world. Decked out, as usual – Prince isn't much for leisure wear – the Royal One casts a wary glance out the window of his car. He doesn't see his privileged domain as a gilded cage. Far from it – it's much safer on the inside. The Artist Formerly Known as Prince is a man who has stringently controlled his music, his look, even his name, transforming himself from a person into a Symbol. Outside the limousine, though, is a world he can't control and has no desire to enter, except when he can set the conditions. Paul Simon evidently feels differently. In Raeanne Rubenstein's photograph, Simon is squeezed to one side of an otherwise empty couch-sized seat, like a kid being sent off to boarding school against his will, a poor little rich boy. Decked out in jeans and a windbreaker – Simon isn't much for formal wear – he casts a sidelong glance, as Prince does. But Simon's look toward the window opposite him is less a nervous appreciation of his solitude than an envious glance at the world outside, the expression of a claustrophobic fear that he is going to be swallowed up by the darkness around him. Rubenstein felt that Simon had the quality of a "little boy lost," and her distinctive portrait isolates that element within him. WITH THE EXCEPTION of paparazzi, photographers who shoot rock stars are conspirators with them. On the simplest level, rock stars are perfect subjects. For one, however disheveled they may sometimes appear, they are obsessed with how they look – that's one reason male rock stars get along so well with models – and photographers typically want their subjects to look good, or at least interesting. Beyond that, artists often insist on selecting – or helping to select – the people who will photograph them, ensuring at least a certain amount of camaraderie. And, beyond that, artists often seek "photo approval" from publications – that is, the ability to determine which images taken by the photographer they chose in the first place will be seen by the world. In a context over which rock stars are able to exert so much control, you'd think they'd always be content and cooperative. So why would they give the finger to the camera, as Johnny Cash and Kurt Cobain do a generation apart? Is it just another example of a rebel posture, a knee-jerk exercise of the ability to insult and provoke? Or is it something else? Who or what are they giving the finger to? Is it the photographer? That's unlikely – if they felt that negatively about someone they were working with, the artists would probably just walk out of the session. Is it their audience? That's even less likely, at least in these two cases. Both Johnny Cash and – while they existed – Nirvana expressed a strong degree of identification with their following. So what's the problem? What they're doing is giving the finger to the very process

of having their picture taken, the entire process of creating images, defining a look, that drives popular culture. It is widely known that people in certain indigenous cultures fear having their picture taken, fear seeing images of themselves reproduced. In their cultures, creating images is a serious business, a means of creating a desired reality. They do not create images of themselves conquering in battle or the hunt because they look cool; they are a kind of prayer, a vision they want and need to make real. Unlike indigenous tribes, celebrities in our culture do not believe that their souls will be trapped in the camera or in the photograph. They are afraid of losing their souls and their selves to the machine, though – no matter how ardently they may have sought the warming gaze of the public eye. They understand how important images are in our culture and, more to the point, they understand that they will never fully be able to control that power. They can limit the number of photo sessions they do or even refuse to do photo sessions. They can insist on selecting the photographers who will shoot them (interesting term, that) and insist on photo approval. But images are slippery, particularly in a culture as visually promiscuous as ours. They will escape the most arduous efforts to control them. Even if, like Johnny Cash, you are a straight-shooting guy who doesn't want to have an image, that is your image. Even if, like Nirvana, you are an underground band that doesn't want anything (or at least not much) to do with the image-making machinery, that is your image. There is no getting around it. So artists rebel and give the finger: "I am not only what you are looking at. I am not a look or an image. I exist in three dimensions, not two. I am a human being." BUT THERE IS NO END to the making of many images, the shaping of the look. The media has become a fun-house mirror, and, after all, identity is not fixed; it changes with time and mood and circumstance. The boundaries of the self fluctuate and blur, mix with everything else around, then turn, and turn again into something new. Photographic images are points in that ever-ongoing process. Neither a trap nor an eternal definition, they are the expression of a moment, the capturing of a visual instant, the preservation of something that is inherently impermanent for the ages.

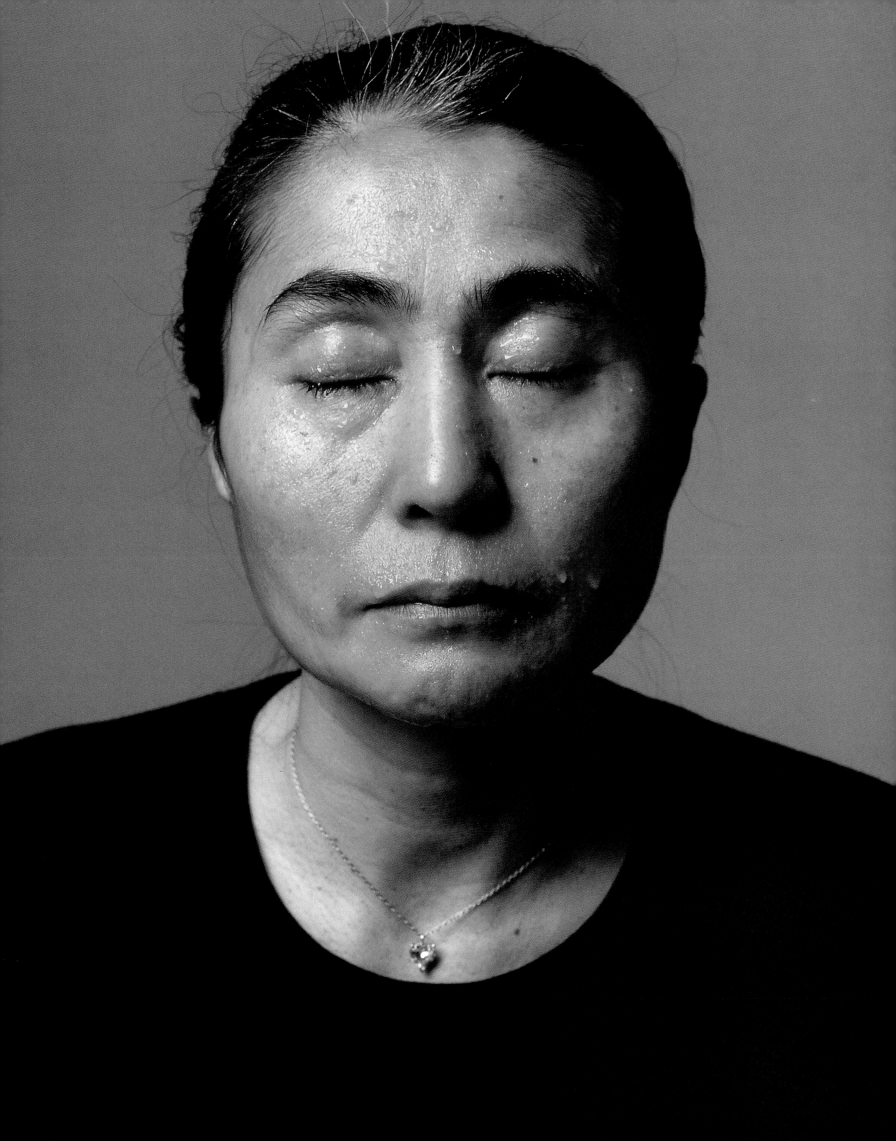

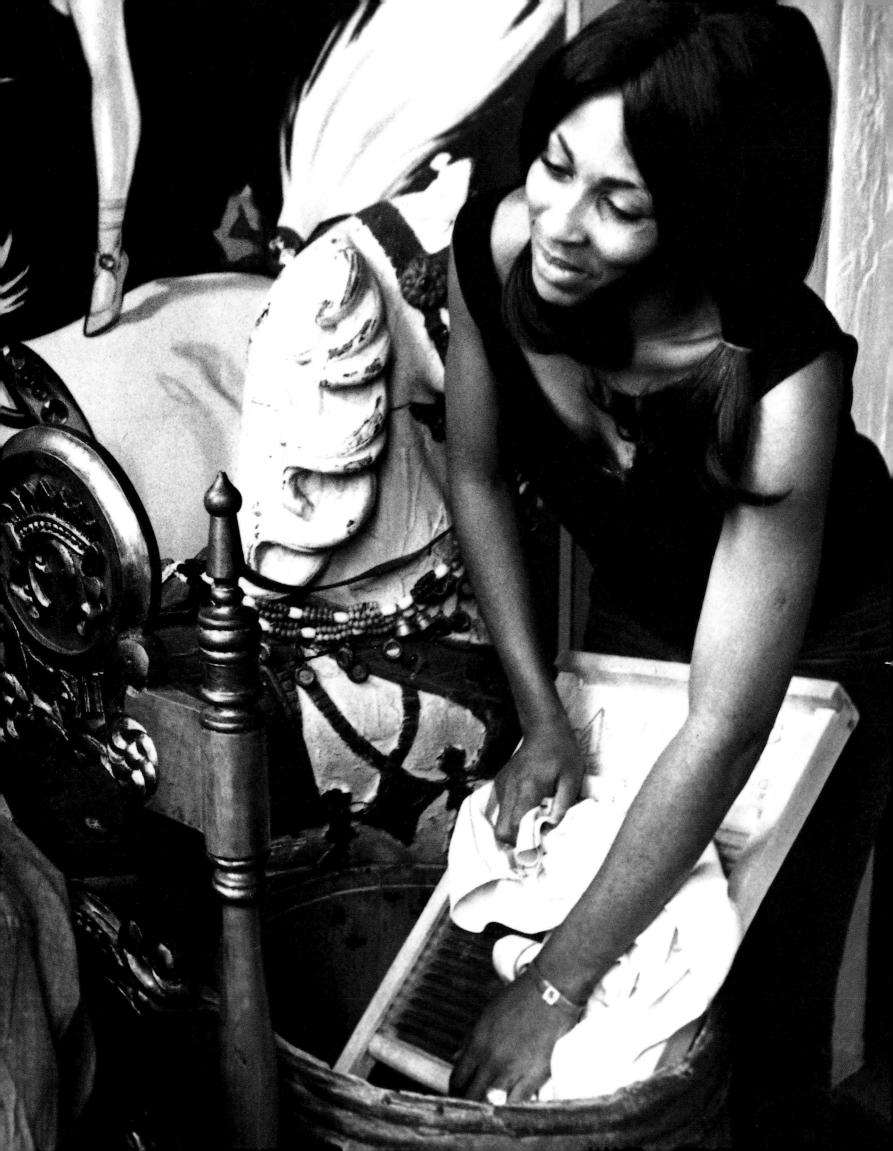

IN SID VICIOUS'S VERSION of punk, anger
To set yourself apart, you punish your body, mutilate
against the world is turned against the self – and the
it; it is a prison and, ultimately, you want to set your-
body as the most visible and most accessible manifesta-
self free of it. Art becomes, in part, a kind of vandalism
tion of the self. In this view, the body is a trap, just like
of the body; a wound, a scar, a kind of savage beauty
the other traps a bankrupt society sets in your path, and
that connects you to others of your desperate tribe
the pleasures of the body are a bribe, a means society
who are similarly marked. Your willingness to damage
exploits to try to make you conform, to become indistin-
yourself offers proof of your commitment and even
guishable from everyone else. Sex (as the portrait of Sid
consolation: No one can ever treat you worse than
handcuffed to his girlfriend Nancy Spungen attests) is a
you are willing to treat yourself. You conquer enemies
form of bondage. The purpose of drug use, if drugs are
by internalizing them and, in your willingness to
used, is to numb pain, not to experience revelation.
destroy yourself, you release yourself from their clutches.

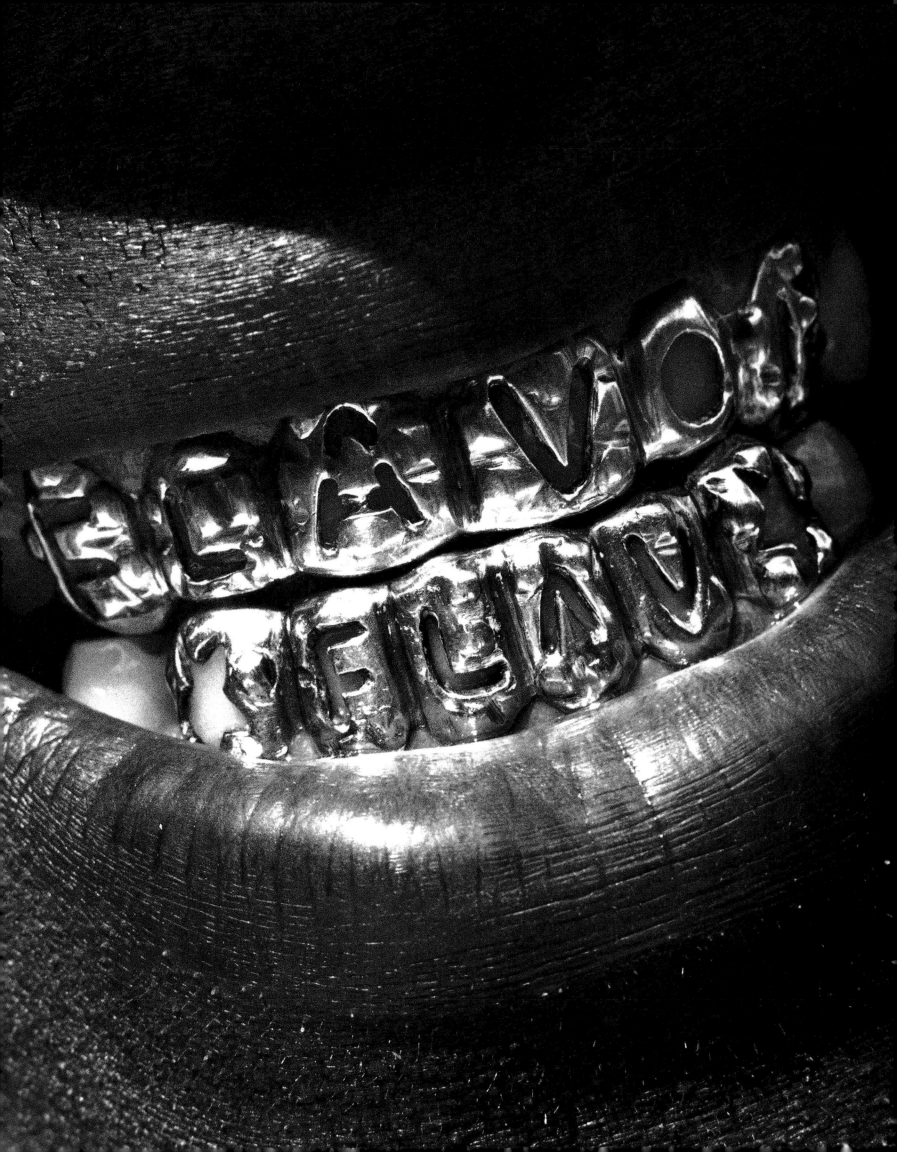

PHOTOGRAPHERS have access to times and places in the lives of artists that we do not, and it's a kick to sneak inside with them. Images caught at such times can document the crafting of an image, the act of refining in private the version of the self that will be presented to the public. That activity can be cynical or manipulative – or it can be a process of discovery, a means of experimenting with possibilities, a justification of the conviction that identity is not fixed but endlessly malleable, subject to our desire to make who we are who we want to be.

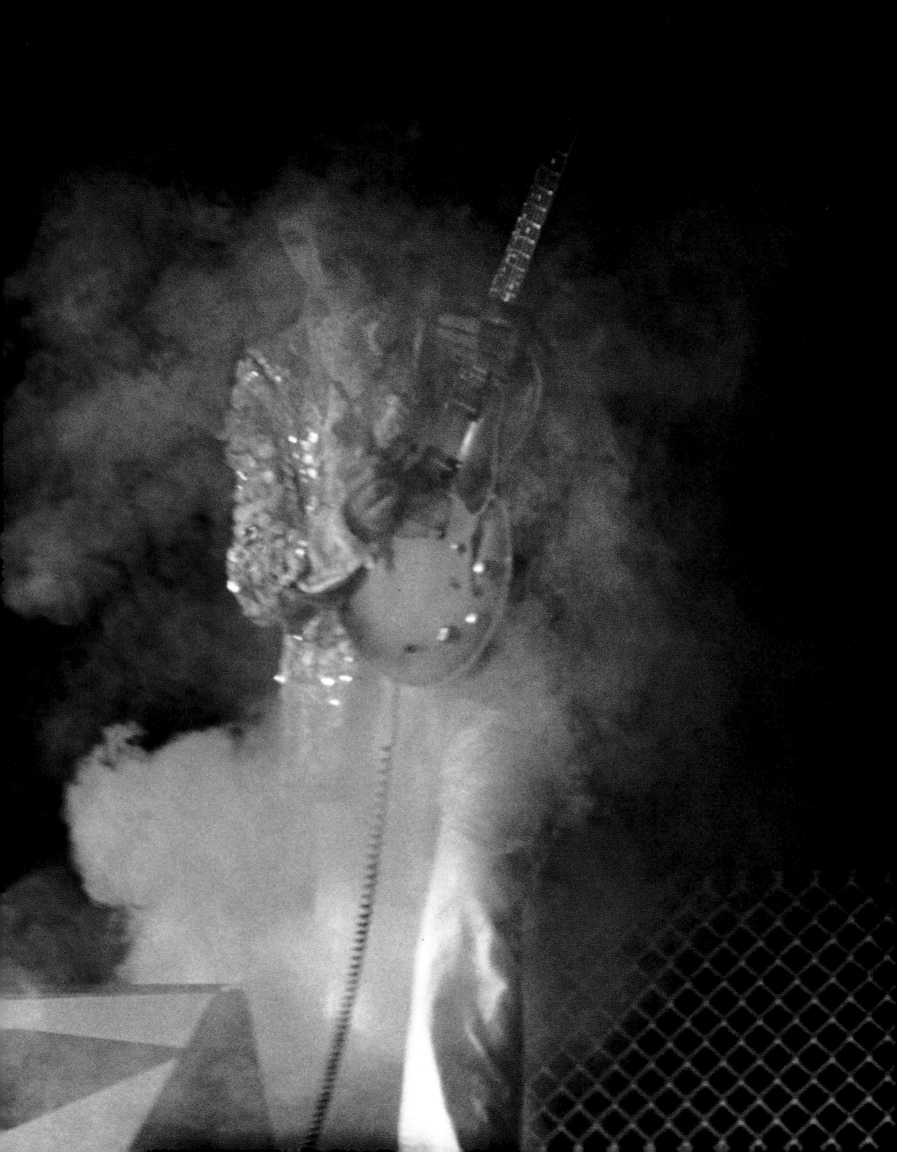

CLOTHES AND PROPS and makeup and faces can tell stories – one look at Peter Gabriel transforming himself before going onstage demonstrates that. Does Gabriel view himself as a warrior preparing to enter battle or a clown whose purpose is to entertain a jaded public? Rock stars are a bit of both, and their performances both pander and assault, flatter and challenge. Makeup enhances and disguises, making a theater of the face and body, transfiguring a person into a character. Life becomes larger than life; the performer is himself and someone else, a man and a metaphor, a person and a commentary. The element of artifice is part of the performance to come, part of the medium through which the artist and the audience engage.

VIDEOS, for better or worse, are now the primary visual medium for rock & roll, not movies, not photographs.

A VIDEO CAN HAVE that kind of commercial impact. A photograph cannot. So what, then, can photographs tell us that videos can't? For one thing, a photograph is about a moment. It's not about a song – or selling a song. Any message a photograph sends about an artist's work is secondary; its primary message is about who we believe that artist to be, how he or she wants to be seen, how the photographer perceives that person. For the artist, the photographer and the viewer, a photograph is a journey into the self. The moment captured in a photograph can be about the whim of an afternoon or the heart of an artist's vision.

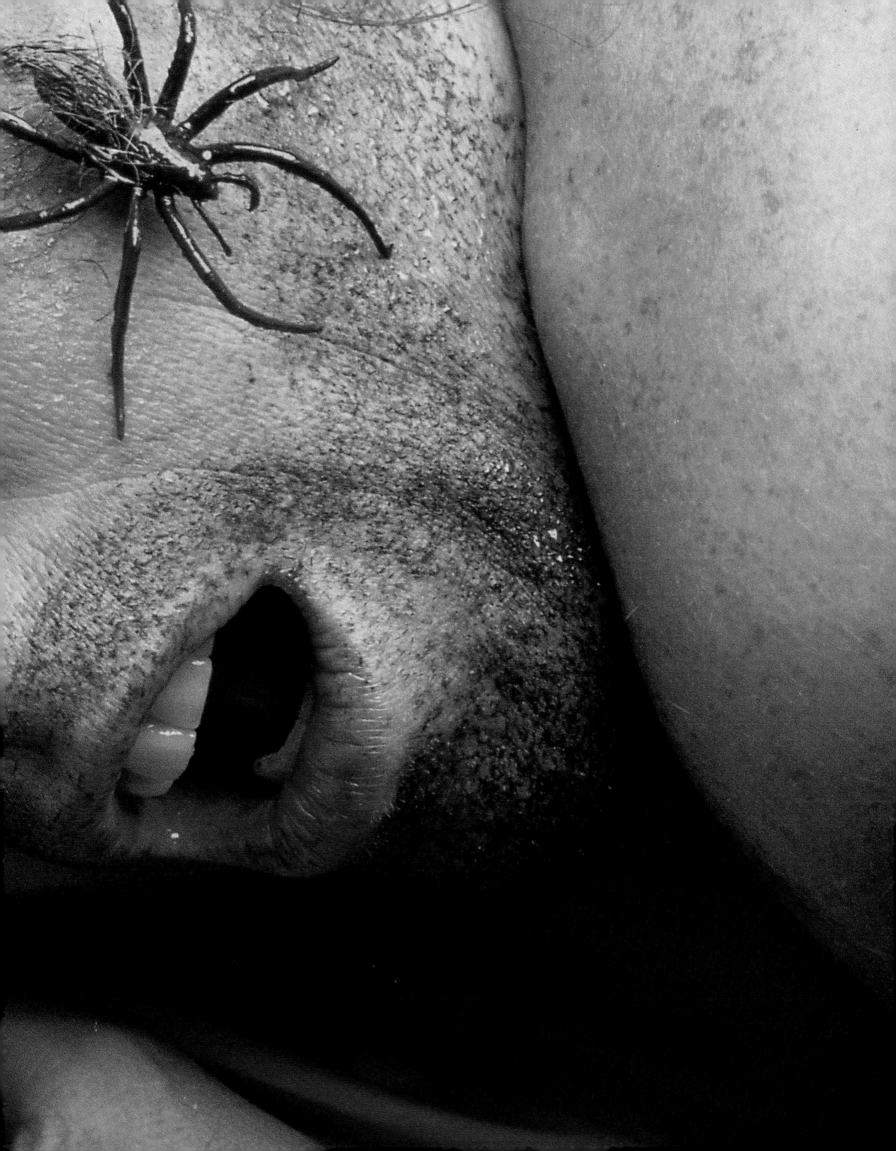

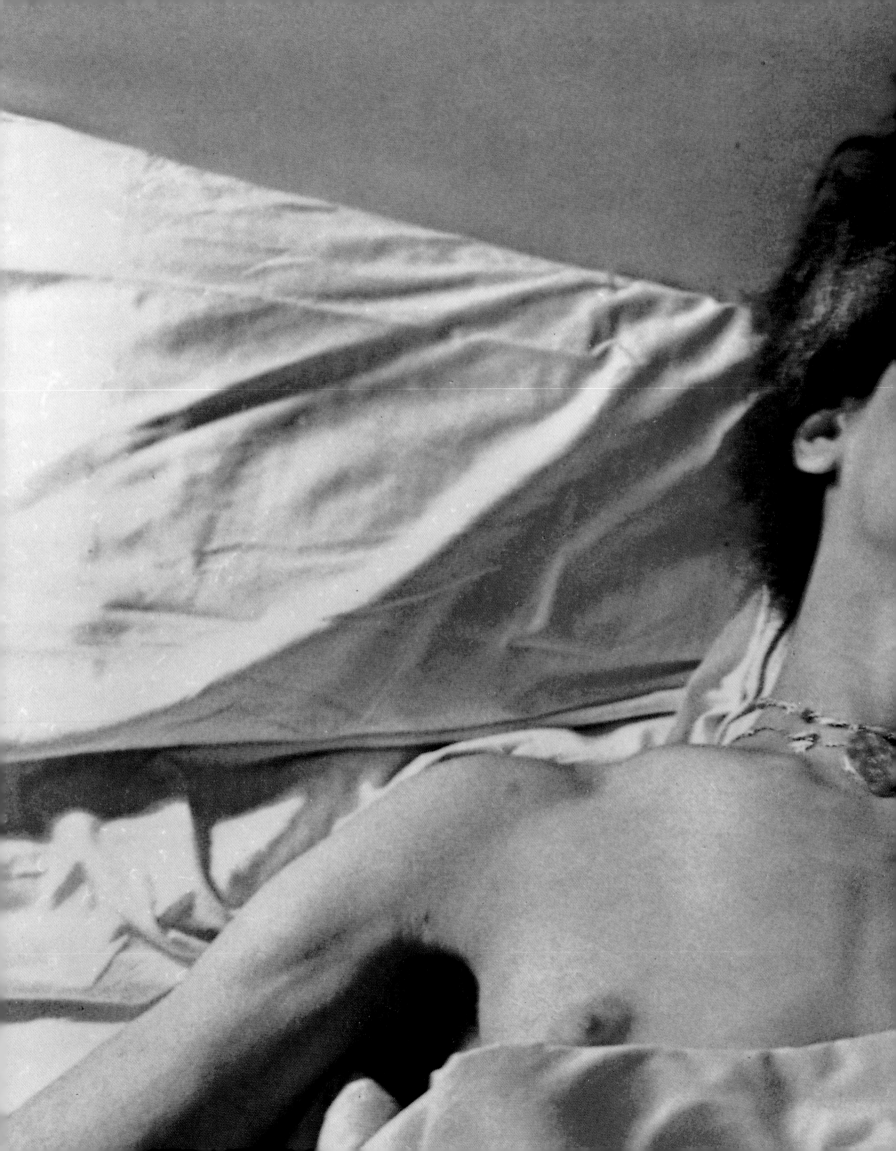

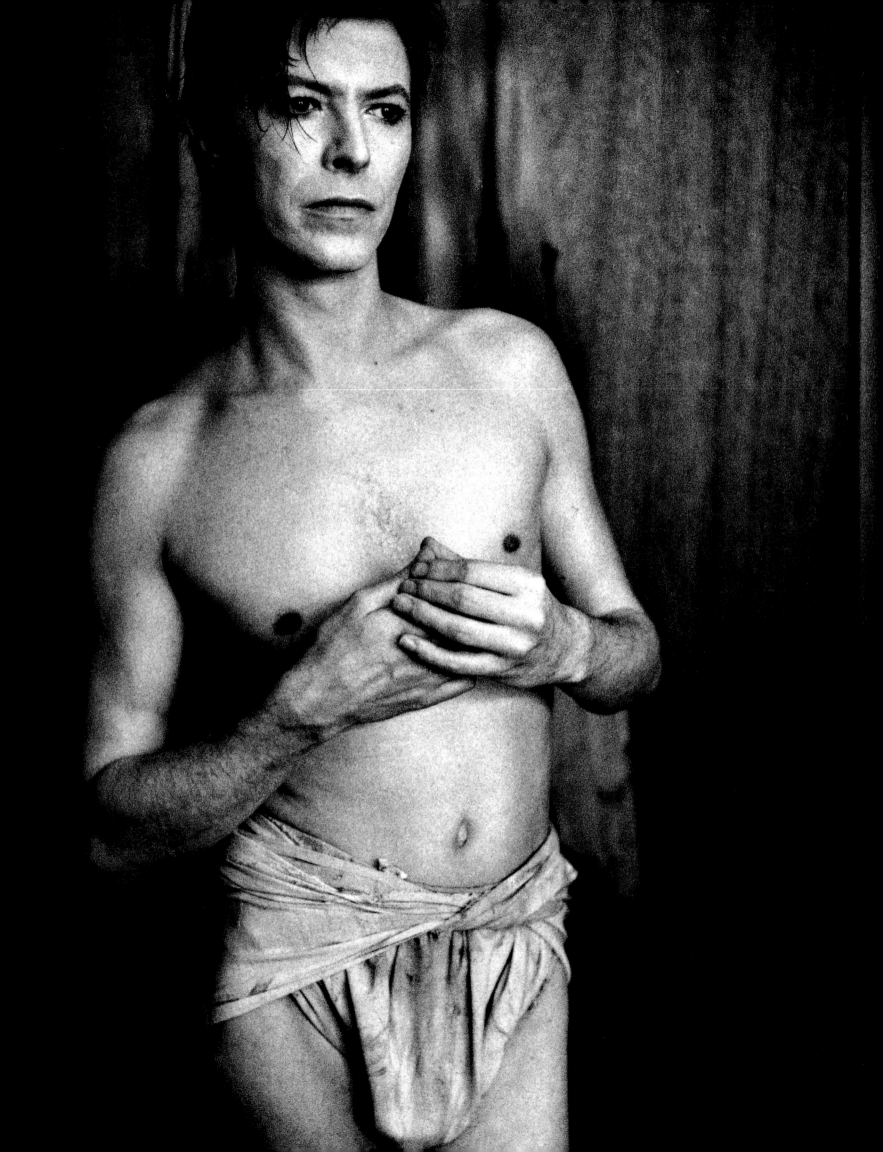

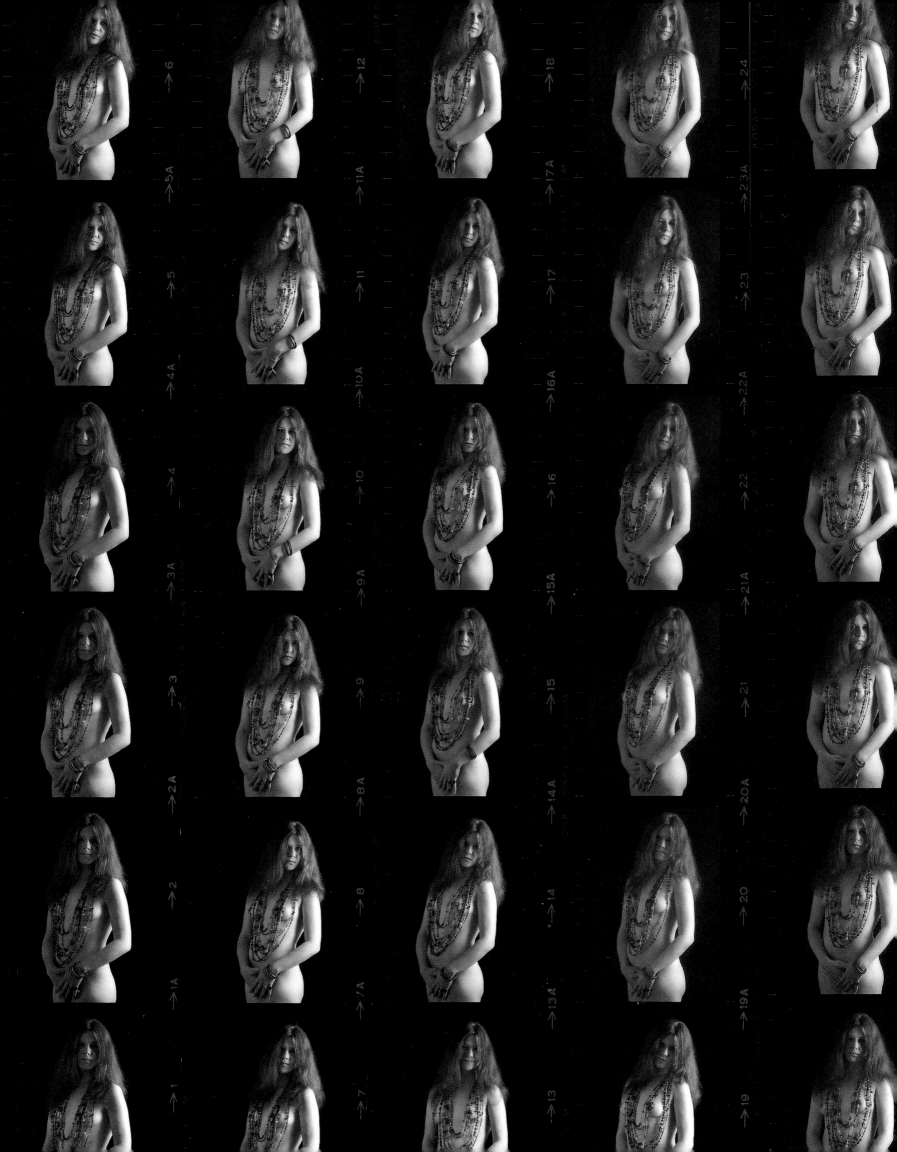

THE HIP TRAPPINGS of success – a fancy car, a limousine, a private jet – are all accessories of the rock & roll image. Lusting after the stuff has never been cool – rappers excepted, of course – but enjoying the stuff has always been. Rockers must never appear to be aspiring to success as artificially defined by the society at large; the symbols of their success must suit them exactly, must seem to be quintessential expressions of their personalities. They must also seem to have been gained on the artists' own terms and no one else's. For one artist it could be the perfect sports car of teenage dreams. For another it could be a lucrative record contract or an elegant home, proof that rock & roll can be the means of secular salvation, can raise a person from the streets to the heavens of personal indulgence. Fans, meanwhile, regard the material success of their favorite artists as confirmations of their faith. The only unforgivable sins in their eyes are pretension and bad taste.

BUDDY HOLLY sinks into his seat and into his coat after being driven back onto a tour bus by a screaming crowd of young girls in Rochester, New York. What's happening outside the bus is nowhere reproduced in Holly's expression, which is serious and inward looking, a far cry from the optimism and delicate yearning of his songs. He's concentrating, thinking about tonight's show or the problems with last night's. Or maybe he's simply tired, another quotidian reality of the road.

When artists are seen offstage, they are often on the fly, in dressing rooms, airports, hotels, cars, buses – the condition of in between. The road has been a time-honored theme throughout the history of rock & roll, the subject of innumerable songs, the pilgrimage from town to town a combination of excitement and unbearable tedium, the road of excess and the lost highway, a quest and a tiresome ordeal. The rush of performance is pitted against the crushing boredom of life in unrelenting movement or the everyday agony of enforced stasis. The thrilling sense of imminent possibility at the heart of travel struggles against the absence of home. Adoring crowds alternate with excruciating isolation, and drugs and alcohol beckon as the road's great balms. The impulse to engage the audience – and the search for a new audience – is unending, exhilarating and bruising. So like all traveling entertainers, rock stars find the road eventually becomes ingrained within them, an internalized no-place place that haunts them, but that also offers frighteningly seductive comforts: the luxury of meaninglessness, a love affair with the surface of things, the grim ecstasy of escape from all the deepest commitments, the calming decadence of just another night along the road.

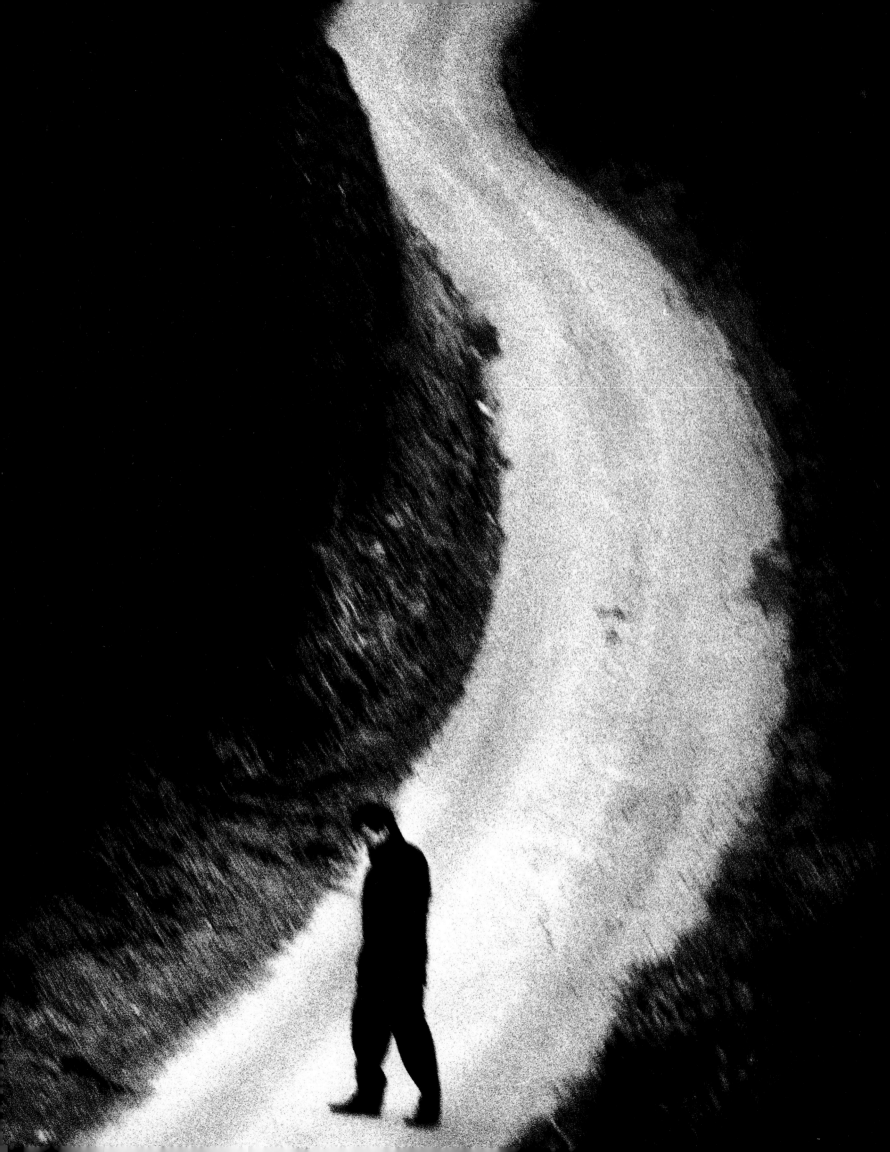

IMAGES can involve the elaborate construction of a persona, metaphor made visible, or they can simply be a minute on the street, an easy instant of posing and moving on, the photographic encounter forgotten the second it is over. The first type of image can entail costumes, historical journeys, a submergence of the self into characters, the evocation in the still photograph of an implied, ongoing drama. The other relies on the viewer's knowledge of the photographic subject; ignorance of the person being shot drains the image of all significance. But are those two approaches ultimately so different? A street is no less consciously chosen as a photographic site than a studio set – even if it is chosen exclusively by necessity. Nor is it any less theatrical. Street clothes are not arbitrary; they are no more or less revealing or concealing of meaning than costumes. Neither is more or less a clue to identity. People smile or laugh in impromptu pictures, not necessarily because they are happy but because they are being photographed. They are playing a role – the role of someone whose picture is being taken – as surely as if they were on a stage.

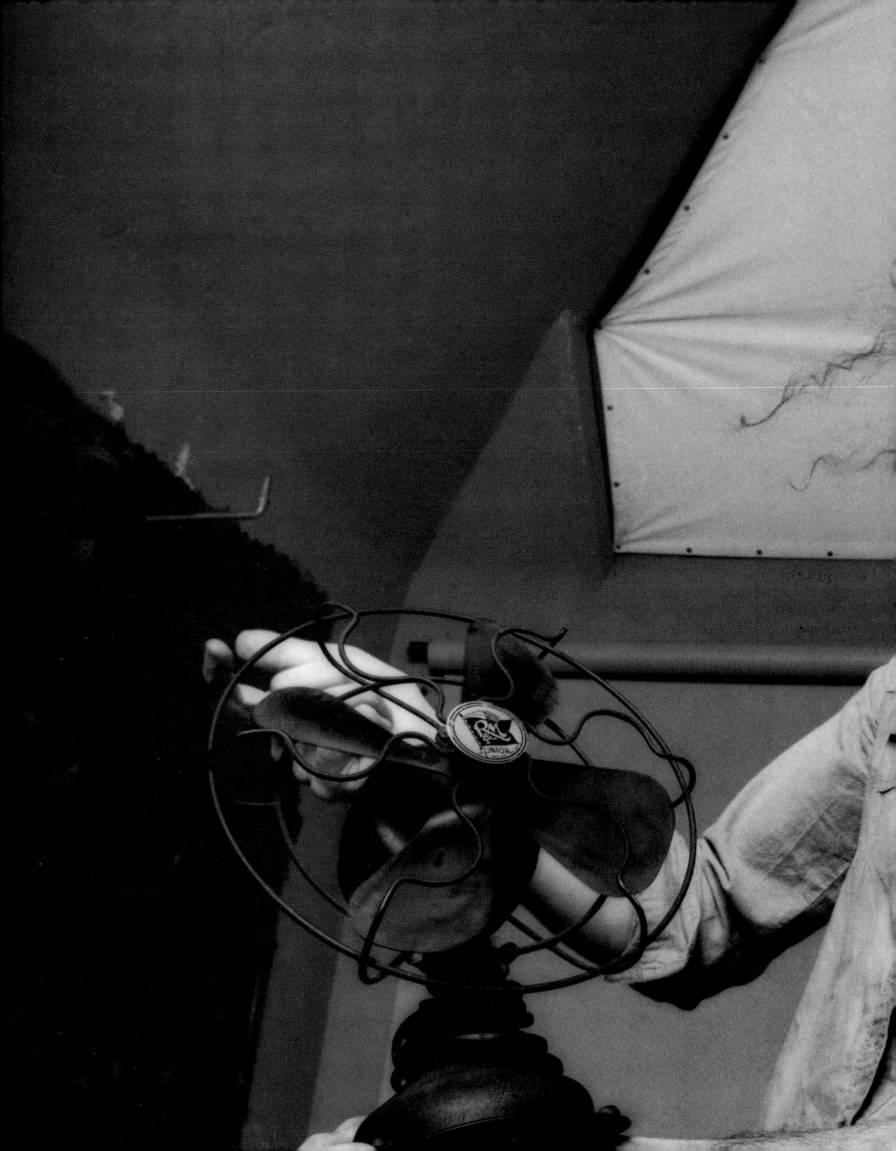

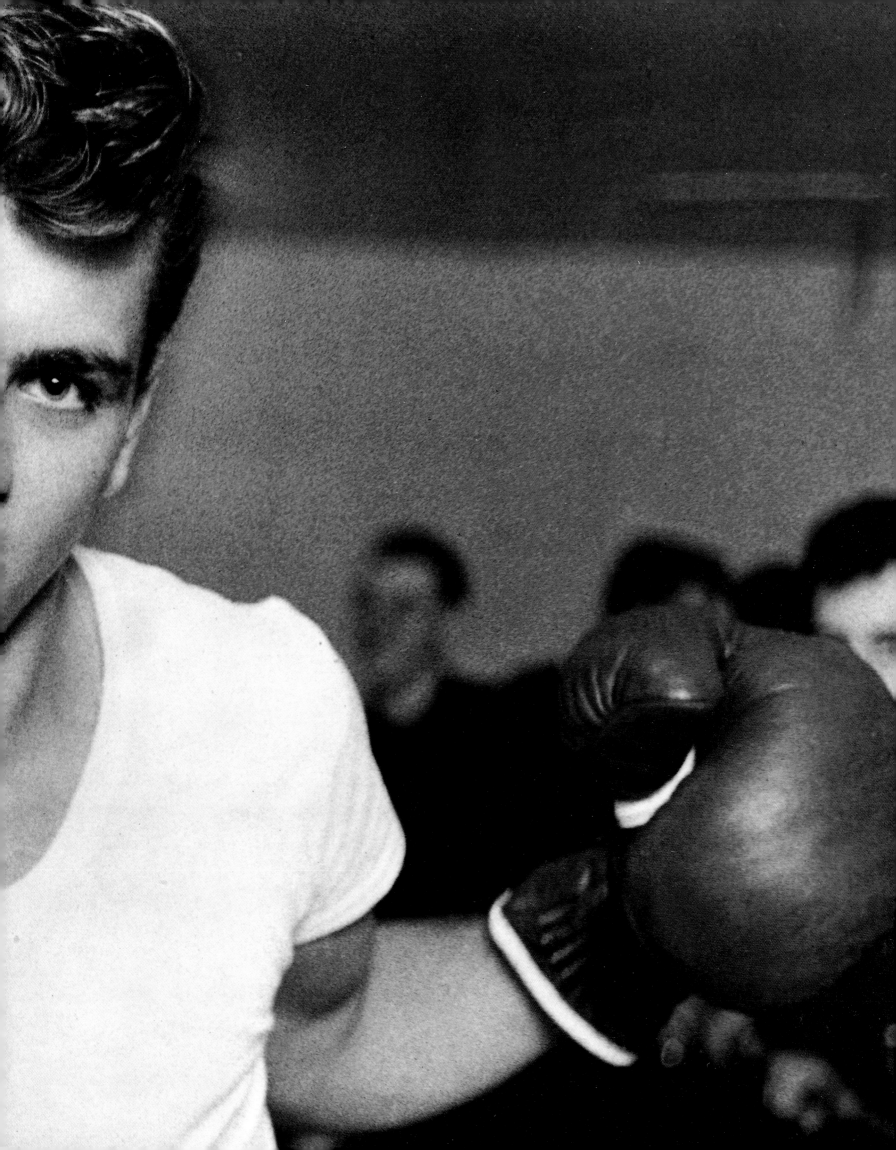

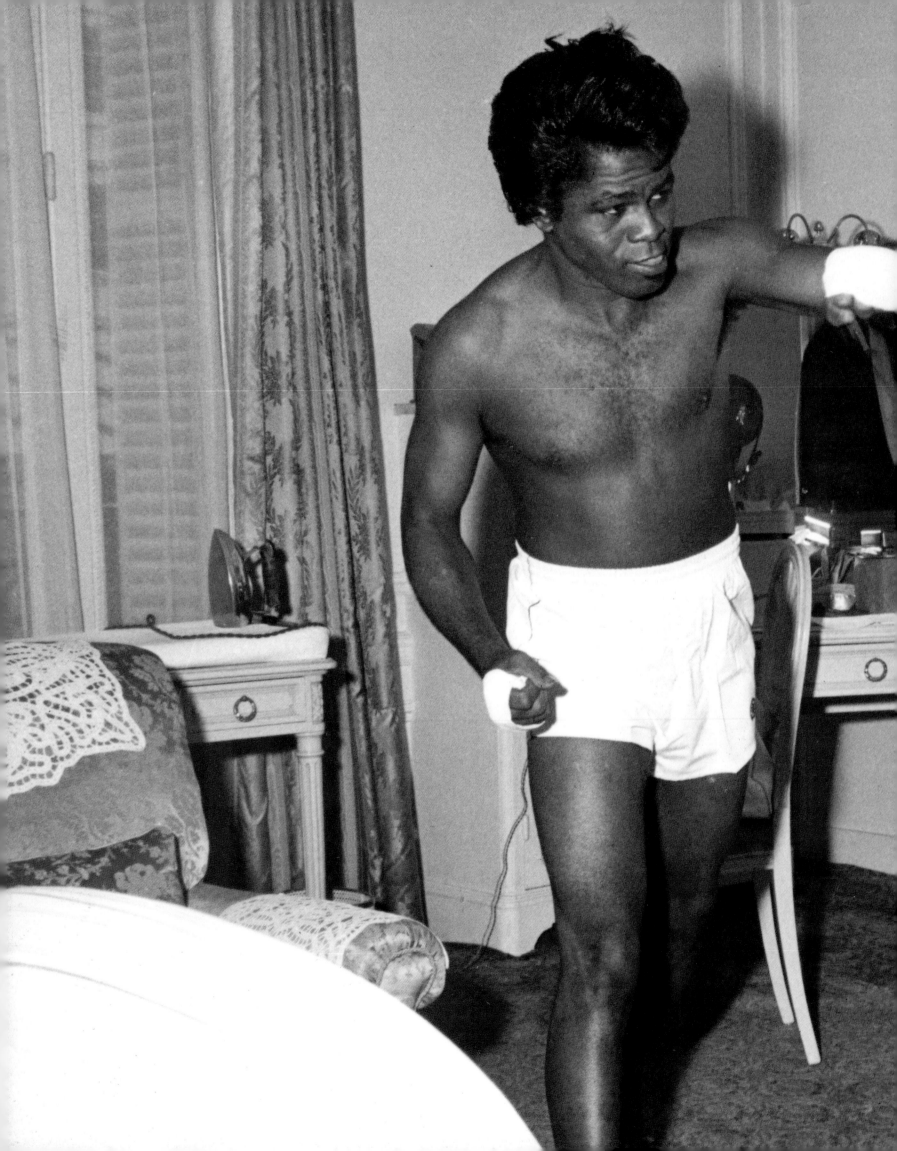

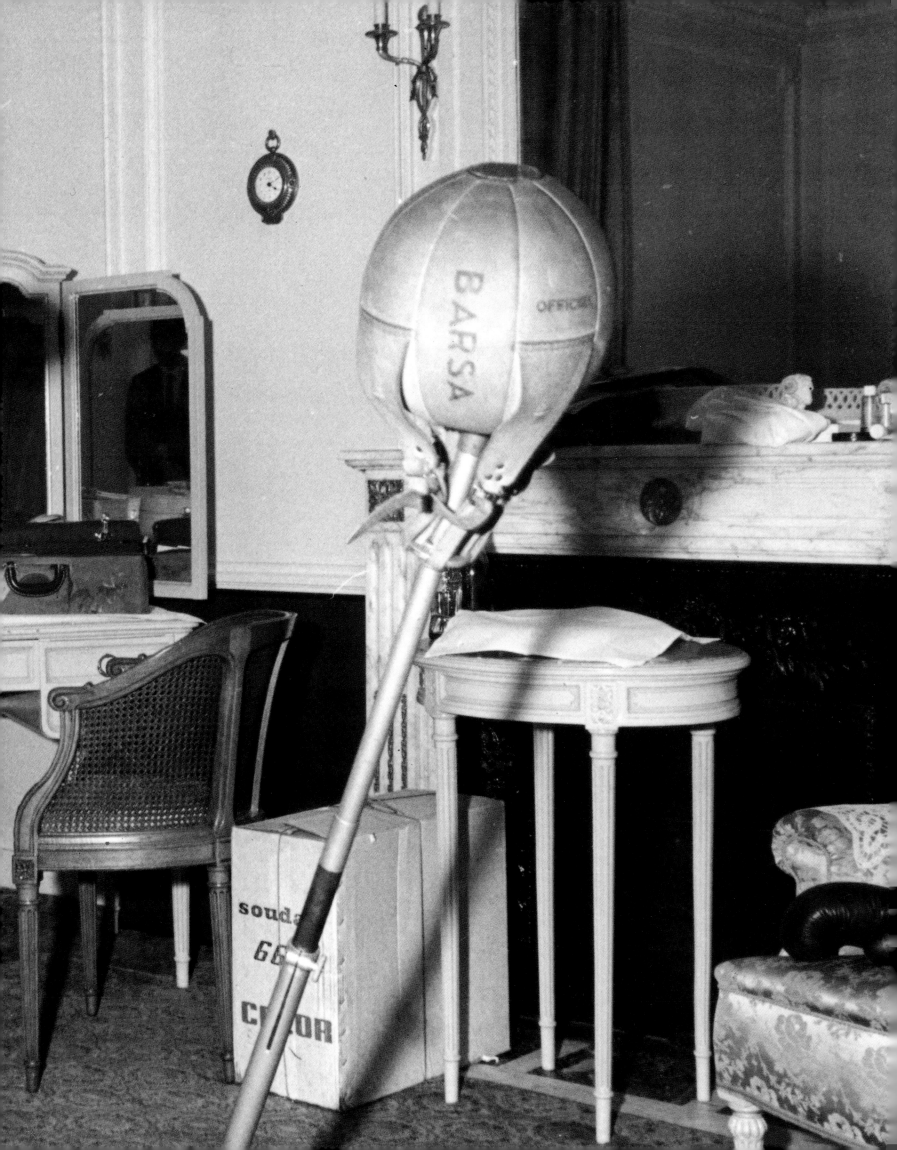

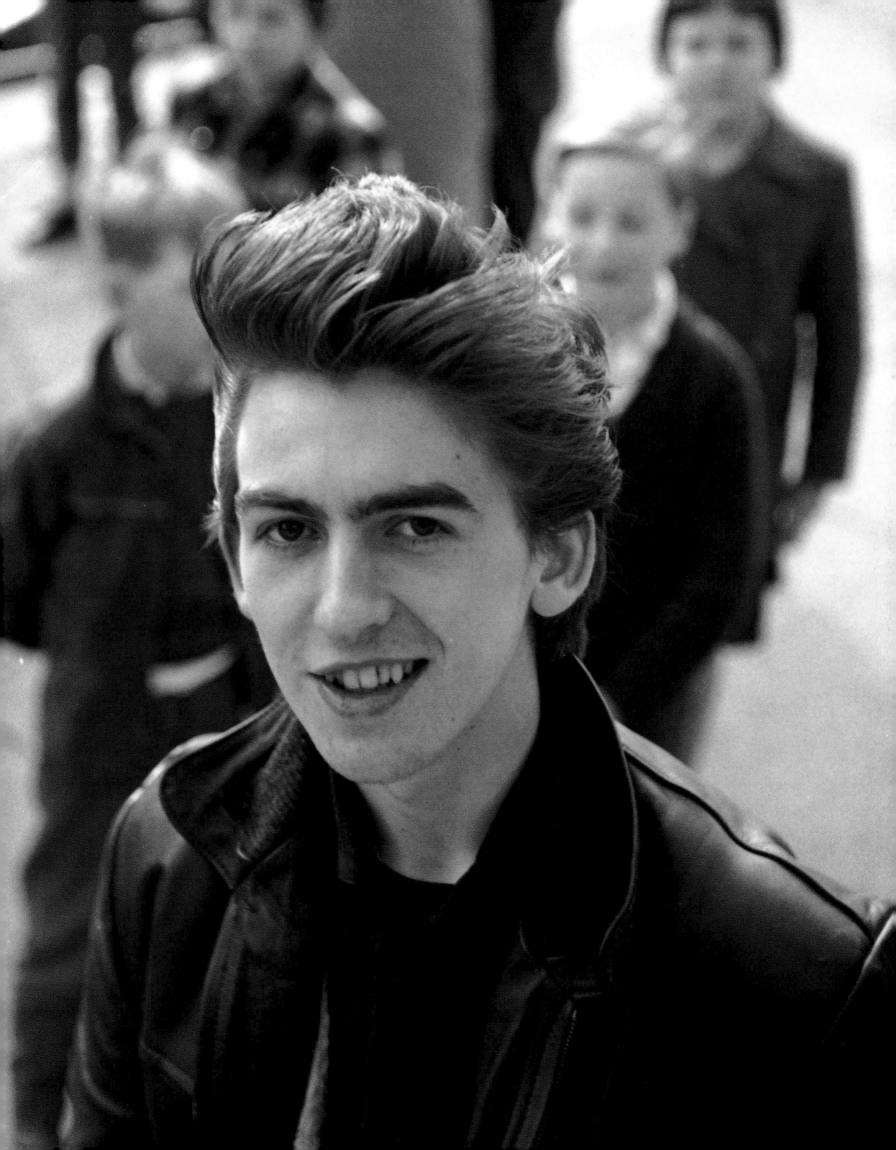

ONCE AN ARTIST permits a trusted

photographer into his personal life, the secret

world becomes known, revelation yields to

the ordinariness of everyday life, and the look

of domesticity becomes as much a part of the

artist's iconography as the most hyped pub-

licity shot. This can be a conscious retreat, as

when the artist who has boldly pressed a

vision upon us steps back and appears to

say, I am just a person. Or it can be a chal-

lenge, pointing out how far from reality we

let these beings live in our imagination.

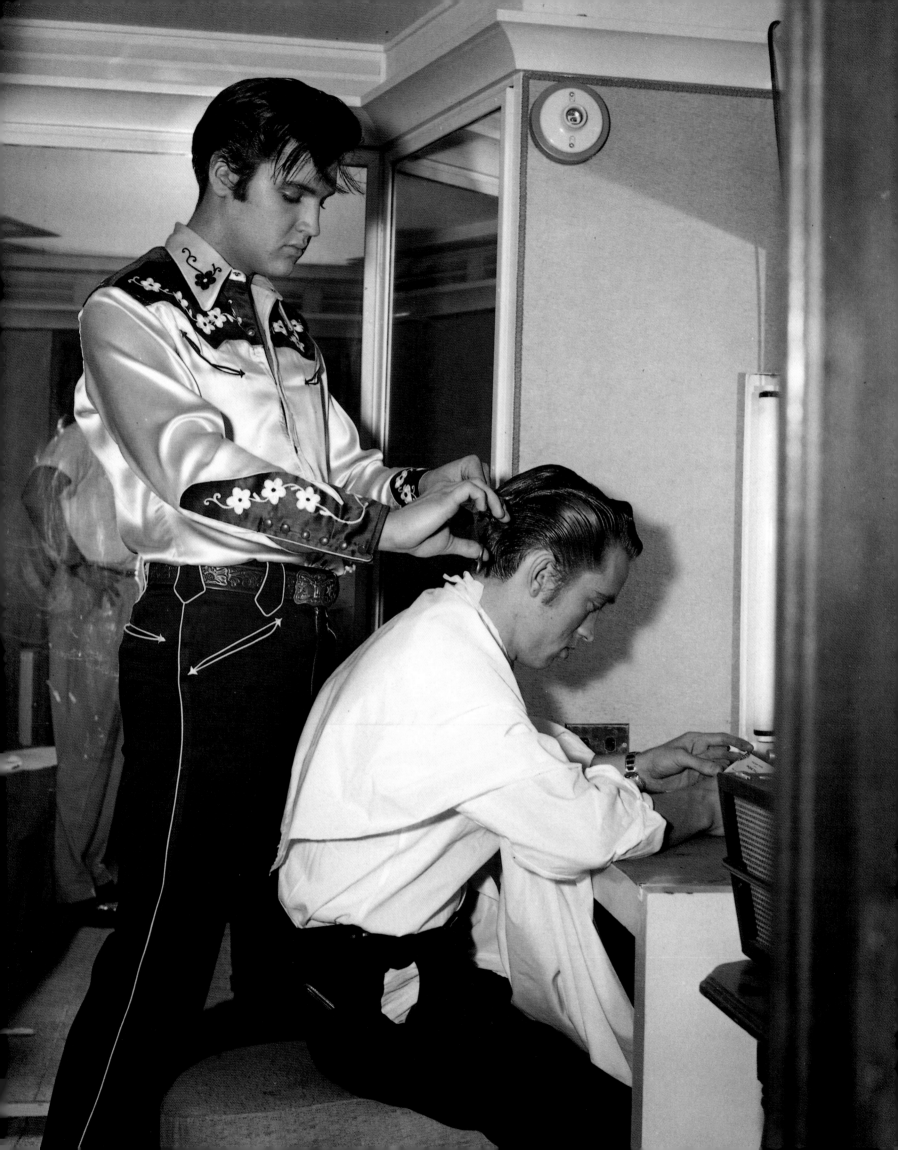

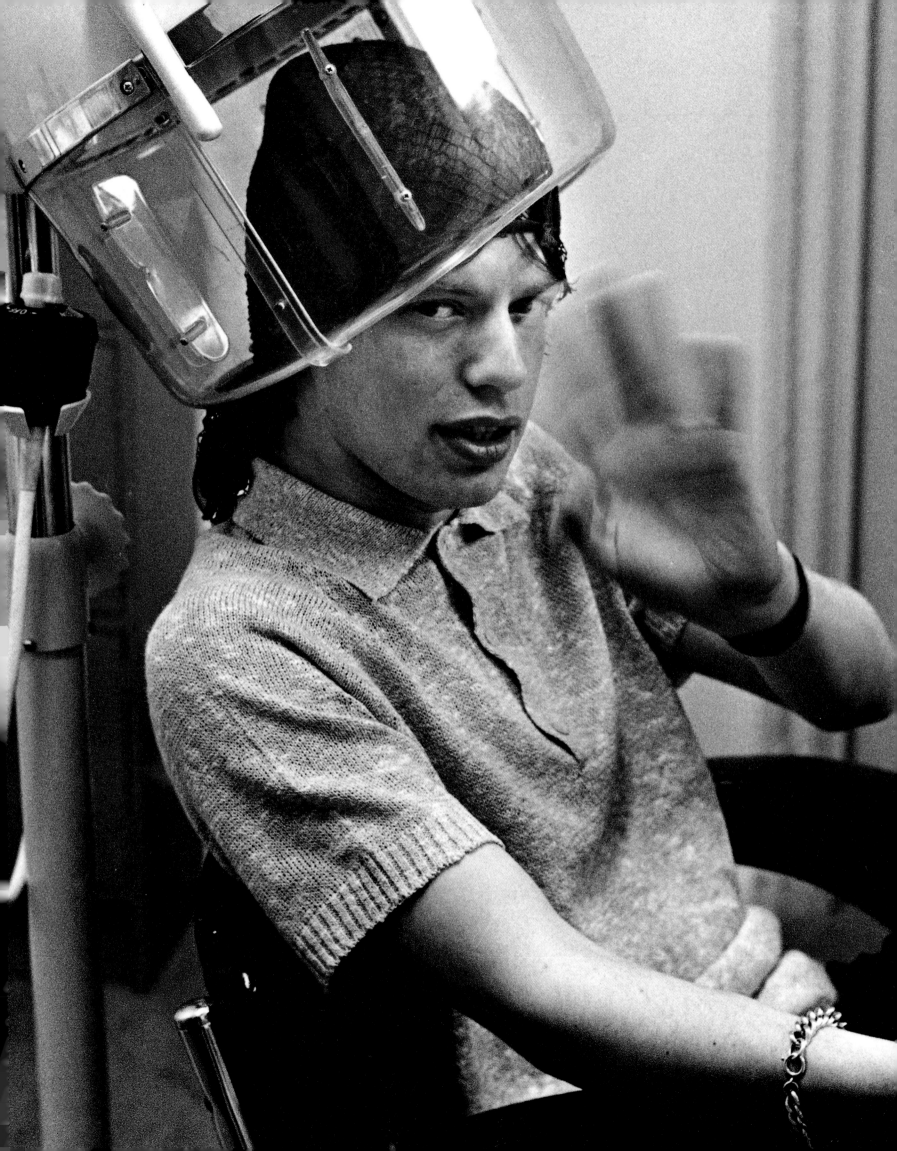

IN PORTRAITS of quiet moments we can sense the explosive drive within artists. *And as we stand in awe of their impressive might onstage, we remember the resonant images of their quieter selves.* Often photographs are also private moments made public, with all the contradictions such a description suggests. *In seeming isolation, the artist is, in fact, twice being observed, first by the photographer, then by us.* To the degree that the artist conspires in the shaping of the shoot, there may even be three levels of observation, with the first taking place in the artist's imagination

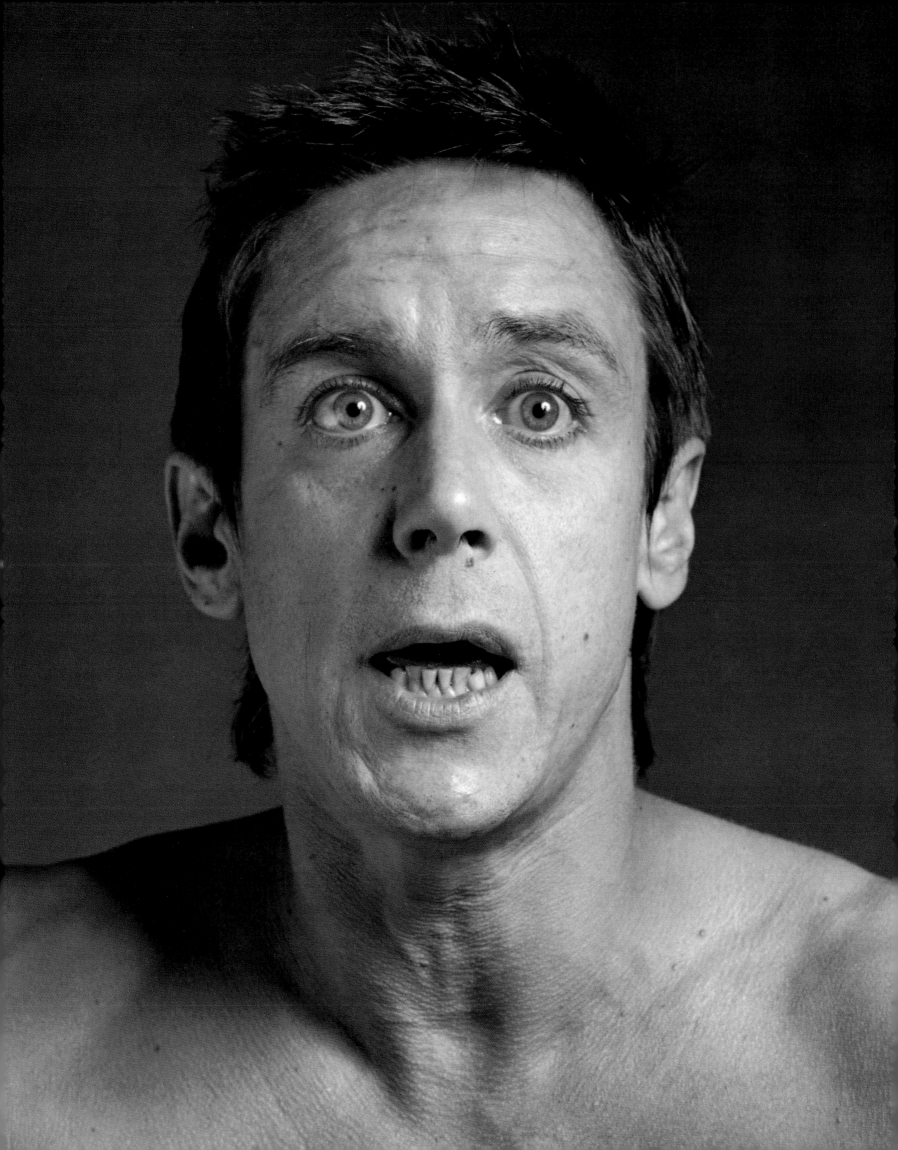

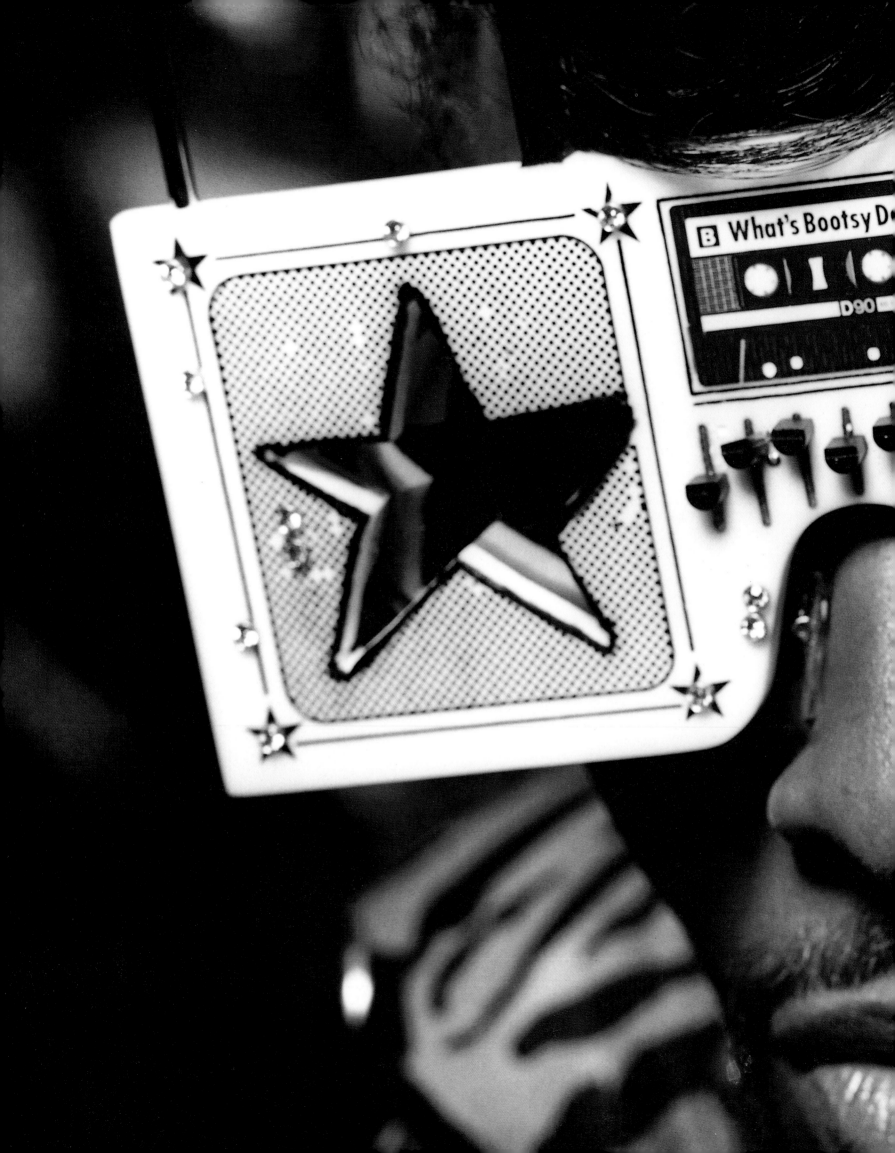

Celebrities in our culture do not believe that their souls will be trapped in the camera or in the photograph—at least not in so many words. They are afraid of losing their souls and themselves to the machine, however willingly they may have sought the warm gaze of the public eye. They understand how important images are more to the point, in our culture, and they understand that, however hard they fully they will never fully be able to control that power.

JOHNNY CASH
Jim Marshall, 1969
San Quentin, California: Marshall accompanied Cash to this concert for prison inmates. While performed on a stage in the mess hall, the show was recorded for *Johnny Cash at San Quentin*. During soundcheck, Marshall remembers shouting to Cash, "Let's do a shot for the warden!" and getting this picture. Cash recalls that his gesture was aimed at a television crew who'd been following him around for three days.

MUDDY WATERS
Terry Cryer, 1958
London: Cryer shot the forty-three-year-old Waters prior to a gig with jazz bandleader and blues aficionado Chris Barber. This was one of the Chicago bluesman's stops on an influential British tour.

MARIANNE FAITHFULL
Gered Mankowitz, 1965
When Mankowitz, who frequently photographed the early Rolling Stones, took this

picture, the teenage Faithfull had already had a hit with "As Tears Go By," cowritten by Keith Richards and future paramour Mick Jagger.

ELVIS PRESLEY
Photographer unknown, 1957
At the height of his initial popularity, twenty-two-year-old Elvis paused on the set of *Loving You* to sign autographs for fans. He would soon be drafted into the U.S. Army. (JEFF CAHN COLLECTION)

STU SUTCLIFFE AND PAUL McCARTNEY
Astrid Kirchherr, 1961
While in Hamburg, Germany, to play a stint on the Reeperbahn, the Beatles had their first professional photo shoot. Bassist Sutcliffe died of a brain hemorrhage not long after leaving the band to pursue his painting career. (STAR FILE)

JOHN LENNON
Astrid Kirchherr, 1962
Hamburg, Germany: The year before the release of the first Beatles album, Lennon was photographed in the art studio of the late Stu Sutcliffe – with whom Kirchherr had been romantically involved. The only light fell from a small window, parting the grieving Lennon's face in half. Lennon and Sutcliffe had been close friends since their student days in Liverpool. (STAR FILE)

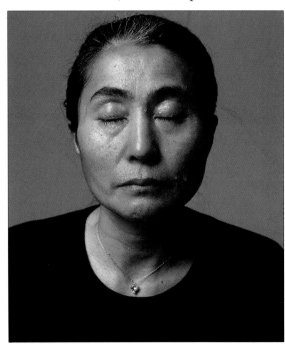

YOKO ONO
Annie Leibovitz, 1981
This was the first portrait taken of Ono following the death of John Lennon. Leibovitz also took the last photos of Lennon before his murder in New York City on December 8, 1980.

ROBERT PLANT; JIMMY PAGE
Herb Greene, 1969
San Francisco: The vocalist and guitarist of the new British band Led Zeppelin posed for Greene during their first American tour. The session was interrupted when the Grateful Dead, "toting guns and live ammo," according to Greene, showed up for an unscheduled photo shoot.

ERIC CLAPTON; STEVE WINWOOD
David Gahr, 1969
London: As the cofounders of Blind Faith – one of rock & roll's first supergroups – Clapton and Winwood were in the midst of recording at Olympic Studio, along with drummer Ginger Baker and bassist Rick Grech. The band began a sold-out – and quite tempestuous – American tour before the album's release; afterward the group broke up. Clapton went on to a solo career, as did his ex–Cream band mate Baker. Winwood re-formed Traffic with Grech before embarking on his solo venture.

IKE AND TINA TURNER
Dennis Hopper, 1966
Los Angeles: Producer Phil Spector arranged for the actor–photographer to do the photo session for the Turners' album *River Deep, Mountain High*. This picture was used for the back cover of the LP, which was a surprise flop, prompting the embittered Spector to go into a two-year seclusion.

JAMES TAYLOR
Norman Seeff, 1969
Martha's Vineyard, Massachusetts: Seeff arrived for the photo session to find Taylor, who had yet to have a successful album, working on the frame of his house.

CARLY SIMON
Norman Seeff, 1975
Simon, then married to James Taylor, practiced yoga during the *Playing Possum* cover shoot. This frame immortalized the singer as she rose from one position.

SID VICIOUS AND NANCY SPUNGEN
Photographer unknown, 1977
This promotional photo for the Sex Pistols' infamous debut album featured the bassist and his soul mate. Both were dead less than two years later. (LONDON FEATURES)

LOU REED
Andrew Kent, circa 1974
Santa Monica: Photographing Reed in his *Rock 'n' Roll Animal* phase, Kent recalled the "terror and excitement" of the Velvet Underground founder's stage persona.

JOHNNY WINTER
Norman Seeff, 1970
Los Angeles: In the wake of the blues guitarist's highly successful 1969 self-titled debut album, Seeff framed the twenty-six-year-old Winter "catching his own self-reflection, an outward expression of that inner movement." Two years later, the albino Texan's career would be briefly derailed by his heroin addiction.

JANET JACKSON
Yuri Elizondo, 1993
Taken at Long Beach Airport, this picture "was inspired by the old glamour celebrity shots of the thirties and forties," Elizondo said. "It was shot looking out of an airplane hangar, into the night."

MICHAEL JACKSON
Claude Gassian, 1984
Knoxville, Tennessee: Two years after the release of *Thriller*, the record that broke all records, Gassian longed to get an atypical shot of the King of Pop performing. "I hid one evening in the summer of 1984," the French photographer recalled, "and I continued to shoot photographs after I was authorized to do so – but I only did it to catch Michael Jackson unposed, I swear!"

ELVIS PRESLEY
Bob Moreland, circa 1955
Moreland photographed the young artist on the brink of stardom. During a stint on the Louisiana Hayride and as a member of Hank Snow's C&W package tour, Elvis's moves caused near-riots. In November 1955, manager Colonel Tom Parker negotiated a deal with RCA, which bought out the singer's Sun Records contract for thirty-five thousand dollars. (GLOBE PHOTOS)

K.D. LANG
Stephen Danelian, 1992
Los Angeles: Danelian wanted to avoid a glamour-puss pose when photographing lang around the time of *Ingenue*'s release, the album of sophisticated torch songs that brought the singer massive success. He waited for a rainy day and, using the Holiday Inn in the background, captured on film, Danelian said, "a naturalness and fluidity, two key elements of lang's music."

RAY CHARLES
Jim Marshall, 1960
Oakland, California: Charles, who had just scored a Number One pop hit with "Georgia on My Mind," headlined this concert. That night Marshall introduced the thirty-year-old Charles to influential music critic Ralph Gleason, later a cofounder of ROLLING STONE.

LIGHTNIN' HOPKINS
Jean Pierre LeLoir, circa 1962

Paris, France: Texas-born Sam "Lightnin'" Hopkins began roaming his home state in the late twenties, developing a highly influential country-blues guitar style. Hopkins became one of the most successful rural bluesmen, performing all over the world. LeLoir photographed Hopkins at a Parisian nightclub.

JIM MORRISON
Alan Ronay, 1971

After completing the Doors' *L.A. Woman*, Morrison took an extended leave of absence. Ronay caught up with the Lizard King just before he moved to Paris to live with his wife in seclusion. On July 3, 1971, he was found dead of heart failure.

SNOOP DOGGY DOGG
Dan Winters, 1993

Winters photographed Snoop as he was coming into the public eye. A bit nervous at the beginning of the session, Snoop loosened up when Winters played *The Chronic*, the new album by Snoop's mentor Dr. Dre. Having been a featured guest on the recording, Snoop rapped along with each line. His multiplatinum debut, *Doggystyle*, appeared at year's end, ensuring his place in hip-hop history.

MISSISSIPPI FRED McDOWELL
Baron Wolman, 1969

Memphis: Wolman and fellow photographer Jim Marshall spent the summer of '69 documenting music festivals, such as this blues fest where he caught McDowell backstage. The bottleneck slide guitarist made his name playing Mississippi juke joints but was actually born in rural Tennessee.

B.B. KING
The Hooks Brothers, 1949

Still known by his given name, Riley King, the blues guitarist had just moved to Memphis when this picture was taken at a Beale Street portrait photography studio. Living with his cousin bluesman Bukka White, King would soon become a famous WDIA radio DJ, gaining the nickname "Blues Boy," later shortened to B.B. (MICHAEL OCHS ARCHIVES)

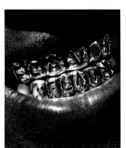

FLAVOR FLAV
Jesse Frohman, 1992

New York City: Cruising on the momentum of Public Enemy's immensely popular albums – 1990's *Fear of a Black Planet* and the following year's *Apocalypse '91 … The Enemy Strikes Black* - jokester Flavor Flav reminded Frohman of "James Brown on speed." Frohman found the gold caps on Flav's teeth so indicative of the rapper's character he saved the last few frames of the shoot to capture them on film.

ARETHA FRANKLIN AND CHOLLY ATKINS
Photographer unknown, 1961

Choreographer to most Motown acts, Atkins also worked with nineteen-year-old Franklin, then signed to Columbia Records and singing pop ballads. Several years later she moved to Atlantic Records and created the megahits that came to define soul music. (FRANK DRIGGS COLLECTION)

JACKIE WILSON
Photographer unknown, circa 1958

Considered the most amazing live performer in rock & roll, Wilson, dubbed Mister Excitement, influenced other dynamic showmen, including James Brown. At this show, Wilson was the headliner of a rock & roll package tour that traveled the United States in the late fifties. (MICHAEL OCHS ARCHIVES)

MADONNA
Peter Lindbergh, 1994

Madonna briefly studied dance at the Graham School when she was eighteen. Here, she tries out moves inspired by Martha Graham for a fashion magazine article, in which she wrote of her "camaraderie" with the dance legend's "pioneering spirit and rebellious creative energy." (HARPER'S BAZAAR)

ELVIS PRESLEY
Jean Cummings, 1956
Tupelo, Mississippi: After Elvis's sensational appearances on several TV variety shows, including those hosted by the Dorsey Brothers, Ed Sullivan and Steve Allen, his hometown honored him with Elvis Presley Day. (FLOWER CHILDREN)

PATTI SMITH
Bill King, 1975
Smith, a whirling dervish in performance, had just released her debut, *Horses*. Her inspirations were equal parts Stax/Volt soul, sixties girl groups, the Rolling Stones, Jim Morrison, Bob Dylan and Arthur Rimbaud.

JERRY LEE LEWIS
Photographer unknown, circa 1965
By the mid-sixties, with his early hits way behind him, Lewis toured the club circuit relentlessly, billing his act "the greatest show on earth." This image, taken at a typical Lewis venue, was a promo picture from that time. (Note the strange Pippi Longstocking legs above the Killer's head and the empty beer bottle at his feet.) In 1968 Lewis abandoned rock & roll for C&W.

CHUBBY CHECKER
Bill Ray, 1959
Ray captured eighteen-year-old Philadelphian Ernest Evans, a.k.a. Chubby Checker, doing the dance he made famous. "The Twist" was actually written and first recorded by R&B singer Hank Ballard, but it was Checker's version that catapulted to the top of the charts, not once but twice – in 1960 and 1962. Checker, who got the idea for his name from New Orleans rock & roll legend Fats Domino, went on to promote several less popular dance crazes: the Hucklebuck, the Fly, the Pony and the Limbo.

ELTON JOHN
Barry Wentzell, 1973
Photographed the year of his *Goodbye Yellow Brick Road*, John was milking his over-the-top stage persona, using extreme versions of shoes and glasses to exaggerate his image. John became the first artist since the Beatles to have four albums in the U.S. Top Ten simultaneously. (STAR FILE)

PAUL WELLER; PETE TOWNSHEND
Pennie Smith, 1978; 1982
A photographer for *New Musical Express*, Smith liked to work close to the stage, never planning a shot but acting on instinct. She knew the performance styles of both Paul Weller *(right)*, then fronting the Jam, and the Who's Pete Townshend *(left)* well enough to sense what they would do. When each made a characteristic jump, she shot. Weller's guitar technique was inspired by Townshend – as were his jumps. The Jam was so influenced by the Mod-era Who that the band was often referred to as the new Who. Weller, then twenty, broke up his band four years later to form the R&B-tinged Style Council. The Who, which originally formed in 1964, also announced that the 1982 tour would be the band's last, but eventually re-formed temporarily for several reunion performances.

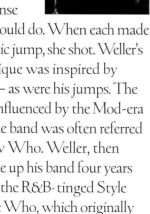

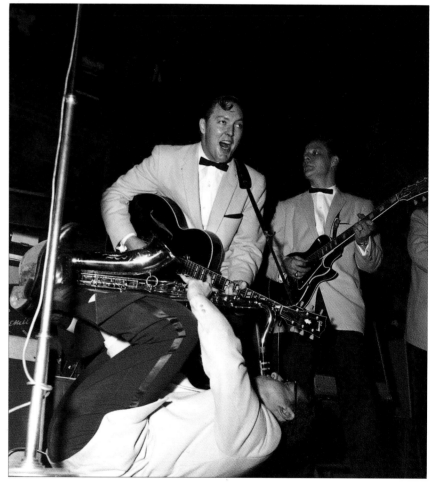

BILL HALEY AND HIS COMETS
Mickey Pallas, 1956
Chicago: The 1955 movie *Blackboard Jungle* sent Haley's "Rock Around the Clock" to the top of the pop charts. Pallas, primarily a jazz photographer, was amused by the mania surrounding the new sound called rock & roll.
(UNIVERSITY OF ARIZONA FOUNDATION/THE CENTER FOR CREATIVE PHOTOGRAPHY COLLECTION)

EDDIE VEDDER
Chris Cuffaro, 1991

New York City: With Vedder's frontman skills well-honed and a debut album in the stores, Pearl Jam had yet to experience superstardom. But by the end of the next year *Ten* had gone multiplatinum. "Music saved me," the lead singer later said. "I mean, my upbringing was like a hurricane, and music was the tree I held onto."

SAM AND DAVE
Photographer unknown, circa 1967

Sam Moore and Dave Prater had their biggest year in 1967 with the classic hit "Soul Man." The duo, nicknamed "Double Dynamite," began feuding, breaking up the first time in '70 – with a final split in 1982.

(MICHAEL OCHS ARCHIVES)

VAN MORRISON
Photographer unknown, circa 1967

Van Morrison had just scored his first hit as a solo artist, "Brown Eyed Girl," after leaving the Irish band Them. (MICHAEL OCHS ARCHIVES)

HOWLIN' WOLF
David Gahr, 1966

Newport Folk Festival, Rhode Island: The great Chicago blues belter, born Chester Arthur Burnett, wowed large audiences – as well as the stage hands. Wolf's bands included such influential musicians as guitarist Hubert Sumlin, pictured here between Wolf and bassist Andrew "Blueblood" McMahon.

TALKING HEADS
Godlis, 1977

New York City: An auspicious moment, this was the Talking Heads' first night as a foursome at CBGB, the club that gave the band, formed in 1975, its start. Ex–Modern Lover Jerry Harrison (*at left*), on guitar, joins original members, drummer Chris Frantz, lead singer–guitarist David Byrne and bassist Tina Weymouth. Their debut album, *77*, was released on Sire later in the year.

STEVIE WONDER
Popsie Randolph, 1963

Randolph shot a performance by the thirteen-year-old singer at Harlem's Apollo Theatre. Then billed as Little Stevie Wonder, he had just had his first Number One hit, "Fingertips (Part 2)." (FRANK DRIGGS COLLECTION)

BRENDA LEE
Photographer unknown, 1960

With her mighty voice, Brenda Lee's compelling delivery fooled audiences into believing she was far older than her sixteen years. During a tour in France it was rumored that she was a thirty-two-year-old midget. (MICHAEL OCHS ARCHIVES)

IGGY POP
Claude Gassian, 1977

Paris: The former Stooges leader had released his second solo album, *Lust for Life*, in '77. The Igster later wrote in his memoirs: "Once I started playing onstage … it was like a wolf after getting his first blood or something. As soon as I had a taste of that, I just abandoned all interest in *music* and went right straight for the throat."

BOBBY "BLUE" BLAND
Photographer unknown, circa 1958

The patriarch of soul singing, Bland got his first recording contract after working as B.B. King's chauffeur. The Memphis artist has scored over twenty R&B Top Ten singles, beginning with 1957's "Farther Up the Road."

OTIS REDDING
Photographer unknown, circa 1967

Redding gave a stunning show at the Monterey Pop Festival in 1967. Six months later, in one of rock's greatest tragedies, he was killed in a plane crash. (MICHAEL OCHS ARCHIVES)

BUDDY GUY
Photographer unknown, early 1960s
Discovered by Muddy Waters at a Chicago club, Guy remembered: "I started crying, telling him I'm going back home because I didn't know anybody and I was about to starve. He said, 'No, you're gonna play this guitar. . . . I'm here to hear you, and when *I* hear you play, you ain't going no-damn-where.'" (MICHAEL OCHS ARCHIVES)

THE BEATLES
Jim Marshall, 1966
San Francisco: Marshall, the official photographer to shoot the Beatles' final live concert, captured the Fab Four – John, George, Paul and Ringo – heading for the stage that evening of August 29th in Candlestick Park.

KISS
Barry Levine, 1978
New York City: Levine wanted to use Kiss's Big Apple associations as a theme for this publicity photo, so the group headed for the observatory of the Empire State Building. All made up with nowhere to go are *(from left)* drummer Peter Criss, bassist Gene Simmons, guitarist Ace Frehley and *(top)* guitarist Paul Stanley.

MICHAEL STIPE
Dennis Keeley, 1991
Taken during the video shoot for "Losing My Religion," this photo captured, for Keeley, the R.E.M. vocalist's eccentric nature and "the quiet place he often creates around himself."

SINÉAD O'CONNOR
Albert Watson, 1992
New York City: Watson shot O'Connor the year of her controversial appearances on both *Saturday Night Live* and the Bob Dylan tribute concert.

BRUCE SPRINGSTEEN
Chris Walter, 1981
Los Angeles: Springsteen was in the midst of a lengthy tour of sold-out four-hour shows. Knowing that he often came down to the corner of the stage, Walter waited there with a wide-angle lens, hoping to catch an expressive moment. In the background is saxophonist Clarence Clemons. (PHOTOFEATURES)

SADE
Dorothy Low, 1992
California: During a video shoot for *Love Deluxe*'s "No Ordinary Love," Low captured thirty-three-year-old Sade in a costume of her own design. The silky-voiced singer – born Helen Folasade Adu in Nigeria – had once studied fashion design in London.

PERRY FARRELL
Kevin Westenberg, 1990
San Francisco: Westenberg caught Farrell at a crossroads in his career. Jane's Addiction had gained commercial success with "Been Caught Stealing." Then, in '91, he founded Lollapalooza and dissolved Jane's. Porno for Pyros ensued in '92.

MICHAEL HUTCHENCE
Julian Broad, 1993
Nice, France: Within the span of a four-hour shoot, Broad says, the energetic INXS lead vocalist managed to be photographed "naked up a tree, swimming in his pool, fencing with a mate and topless by an ivy-covered wall, wearing a kilt."

ROBERT PLANT
Carl Dunn, 1970
Dallas, Texas: Dunn went to the Cabana Hotel (now a minimum-security prison) in hopes of photographing the members of Led Zeppelin, who had played the night before. He snapped a floating Plant.

(PHOTOFEATURES)

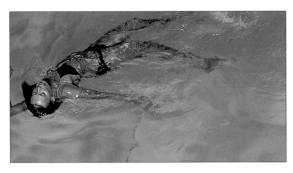

JONI MITCHELL
Norman Seeff, 1976

Bel Air, California: When Seeff went to the singer's home, around the time of *Hejira*'s release, the two agreed to photograph Mitchell in her pool. Though Seeff typically shoots his subjects at close range, he climbed up to a balcony, capturing the lithe songwriter from above.

BONO
Anton Corbijn, 1993

New York City: "The Fly," Bono's persona for U2's *Zooropa* album and Zoo TV tour, satirized as well as thoroughly enjoyed the decadent life of a rock star. Bono once said of Corbijn: "Sometimes he can give you a substance you may not have … but are *working* toward."

JIMI HENDRIX
Gered Mankowitz, 1967

With the Jimi Hendrix Experience (including drummer Mitch Mitchell and bassist Noel Redding) already a huge London sensation, Mankowitz was thrilled to meet the guitarist.

BOB MARLEY
Dennis Morris, 1975

As reggae's leading ambassador – whose songs of determination, rebellion and faith were embraced by fans all over the world – Marley lived and expressed the culture that surrounded the music: ganja, dreads, joy and ease.

BRYAN FERRY
Albert Sanchez, 1987

In this shoot for *Interview*, Sanchez captured what he felt was a very typical moment for the magnetic singer. Sanchez remarked that Ferry sank "effortlessly into a glamorous, dreamlike state." A different shot from this session was used for the cover of 1988's *Bête Noire*.

PETER GABRIEL
Raeanne Rubenstein, 1982

Philadelphia: Gabriel was snapped backstage at the Spectrum Theater. That same year, he founded the World of Music, Arts and Dance Festival.

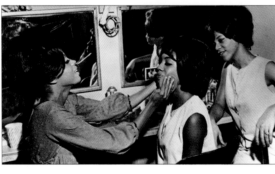

THE SUPREMES
Photographer unknown, circa 1963

While their debut, *Meet the Supremes*, had been causing a sensation, the camera found Diana Ross, already in charge, powdering Mary Wilson's face as Florence Ballard looks on. The Motown singers became the most successful girl group of the sixties. (MICHAEL OCHS ARCHIVES)

CARLOS SANTANA
Joel Axelrad, circa 1973

The Mexican-born guitarist formed Santana in 1967. By '72 he was also working outside the group, primarily with jazz musicians. *Love, Devotion, Surrender*, 1973's collaboration, featured John McLaughlin, Billy Cobham, Stanley Clarke and others. (MICHAEL OCHS ARCHIVES)

PETE TOWNSHEND
Baron Wolman, 1967

San Francisco: For the first concert that Wolman shot for the brand-new magazine ROLLING STONE, he caught the Who's twenty-two-year-old guitarist in a typically agitated moment. After the show at the Cow Palace, editor Jann S. Wenner interviewed Townshend.

DEBORAH HARRY
Roberta Bayley, 1979

Las Vegas: Blondie's lead singer brought a sultry, thrift-store chic to punk rock. Bayley, who first photographed Harry for New York's *Punk* magazine, got her backstage after the chart-topping "Heart of Glass" had sent the band into the big time.

CHRIS ISAAK
Lance Staedler, 1990

The retro rocker, who also has a fondness for fifties fashions, had his Top Ten breakthrough in early 1991 after a version of his "Wicked Game" was featured in the film *Wild at Heart*.

BRIAN WILSON
Annie Leibovitz, 1970

West Hollywood, California: Leibovitz, who started shooting for ROLLING STONE in 1969, photographed the eccentric genius in the aisles of his own health-food store, the Radiant Radish. After 1964, Wilson stopped touring with the Beach Boys and spent more and more time indulging a string of short-lived interests, along with his musical experimentation.

RICKIE LEE JONES
Annie Leibovitz, 1979

Santa Monica, California: The twenty-five-year-old bohemian singer–songwriter had just found success with her self-titled debut when Leibovitz photographed her at home for ROLLING STONE. The album yielded "Chuck E.'s in Love," Jones's only Top Ten hit to date.

JEFF BECK
Baron Wolman, 1968

San Francisco: Wolman captured this intimate moment during a tour of the Jeff Beck Group (which included, at the time, vocalist Rod Stewart and Ron Wood on bass). Guitarist Beck was napping before a performance at the Carousel Ballroom on Market Street (which became Bill Graham's theater, the Fillmore West).

ALICE COOPER
Annie Leibovitz, 1975

With *Welcome to My Nightmare* maintaining his place as the king of "shock rock," Cooper displayed his edgy image. The same year, he starred in a prime-time TV special, played Las Vegas and guested on *The Hollywood Squares.*

JOHN LEE HOOKER
Mark Seliger, 1990

Vallejo, California: Seliger met the septuagenarian bluesman at his home near San Francisco. Hooker went to his closet and pulled out three polka-dot shirts because, he told Seliger, polka dots were his favorite. Earlier that year the Mississippi–born "father of the boogie" was inducted into the Rock and Roll Hall of Fame.

DAVID BOWIE
Michael Putland, 1971

Kent, England: Then a photographer for *Disc* and *Music Echo,* Putland met the singer at his home, where they captured the sexual ambiguity of Bowie's recent album *Hunky Dory,* which featured his virtual theme song "Changes." The next year, after telling *Melody Maker* he was gay, Bowie adopted the persona of Ziggy Stardust, one of several explored in his musical career. (RETNA PICTURES)

ROD STEWART
Ian Dickson, 1974

London: Stewart was apparently sick of "cheesecake" publicity shots, so when Dickson arrived at the Royal Garden Hotel one morning to do the photo session, the singer mischievously climbed into a pair of pajamas his mother had recently bought for him. (REDFERNS)

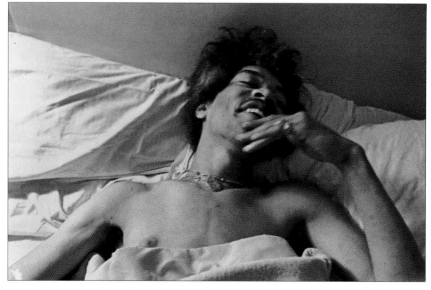

JIMI HENDRIX
Roz Kelly, 1969

This photo caught the twenty-seven-year-old virtuoso guitarist at the peak of his stardom, only a year before his death. Having just woken up, Hendrix reportedly asked the photographer to join him in his bed. (MICHAEL OCHS ARCHIVES)

DAVID BOWIE
Anton Corbijn, 1980

Chicago: A master of imagery, Bowie took the lead in the play *The Elephant Man*. He has said of this photo: "It was a very accurate reflection of me. Very dispirited. Why? 'Cause there's a little Elephant Man in everyone!"

BJÖRK
Laura Levine, 1991

Levine shot Björk – then the Sugarcubes' lead singer – when the band was recording *Stick Around for Joy* near Woodstock, New York. "Like a sylvan sprite," Levine said, the uninhibited Icelandic chanteuse "immediately began peeling off her clothes in the summer drizzle."

THE ALLMAN BROTHERS BAND
Stephen Paley, 1969

From the photo session for the cover of their debut, this outtake of *(from left)* Berry Oakley, Butch Trucks, Jai Johanny Johanson, Gregg Allman, Duane Allman and Dickie Betts was taken near the band's hometown, Macon, Georgia. (MICHAEL OCHS ARCHIVES)

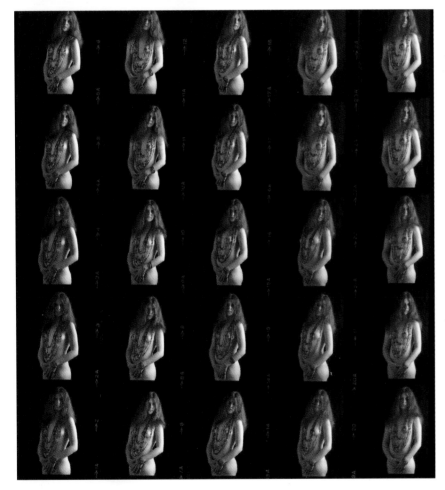

JANIS JOPLIN
Bob Seidemann, circa 1966

Still the lead singer for Big Brother and the Holding Company, Joplin, with her characteristic bravado masking her natural shyness and insecurity, insisted, "Take my picture naked, Seidemann, you motherfucker." One of the frames later became a poster about which Joplin raved in a letter to her family, "I'm the first hippie pinup girl. What a kick!"

RED HOT CHILI PEPPERS
Mark Seliger, 1992

This portrait was originally intended for the cover of ROLLING STONE. As the issue was going to press, guitarist John Frusciante *(far right)* quit the band. So, using a digital process, he was removed (as was some stray pubic hair) from the picture. With Frusciante are *(from left)* drummer Chad Smith, vocalist Anthony Kiedis and bassist Flea (né Michael Balzary).

AXL ROSE
Herb Ritts, 1991

New York City: For the cover of ROLLING STONE, at the time of the concurrent release of Guns n' Roses' two *Use Your Illusion* albums, Ritts photographed the band's twenty-nine-year-old front man in the early morning hours. Though he had anticipated a brief shoot, Ritts said, "Axl kept changing clothes on the set. You just could not resist, you know. His lips and his form, and the fact that he had those symbolic tattoos. It was pretty amazing."

SID VICIOUS
Bob Gruen, 1978

On their very brief tour of the United States, the Sex Pistols were magnets for abuse. At this show in Dallas, Texas, a female fan gestured to Vicious to lean down for a kiss – and then punched him in the nose, causing it to bleed profusely. Reveling in the gore, Vicious spit blood on her. Then he smashed a beer bottle on his amp, using the shards to slash his chest, tearing open a previous (self-inflicted) arm wound. Vicious later reunited with his attacker in a San Francisco love nest where he OD'd and almost died. (STAR FILE)

HENRY ROLLINS
Julian Broad, 1994

Tokyo: Broad caught the thirty-three-year-old singer and spoken-word performance artist as he prepared for a Japanese concert. Rollins, the ex-lead vocalist of Los Angeles–based hardcore band Black Flag, "goes through this yoga-est routine," said the photographer. "Then off he goes."

GENE VINCENT
Photographer unknown, circa 1957
Virginia-born Eugene Vincent Craddock transformed himself into rockabilly cat Gene Vincent after leaving the Navy in 1955. His signature song, "Be-Bop-a-Lula," hit the Top Ten the next year. Touring England with fellow rocker Eddie Cochran in 1960, Vincent was severely injured in a car crash that killed Cochran. Vincent recovered, but his career never regained momentum. (MICHAEL OCHS ARCHIVES)

CREAM
Art Kane, 1967
Philadelphia: Kane squired the members of Cream – guitarist Eric Clapton, drummer Ginger Baker and bassist Jack Bruce – to the railroad tracks because he wanted to depict the "hard-travelin' blues underpinnings" of the band's sound. Due to friction among the members, the trio broke up, giving a farewell concert on November 26, 1968, at London's Royal Albert Hall.

EURYTHMICS
Claude Gassian, 1986
Photographed on a train somewhere between Brussels and Paris, Annie Lennox and Dave Stewart, who were lovers when they first played together in the Tourists, had developed a platonic relationship after forming the Eurythmics.

PAUL SIMON
Raeanne Rubenstein, circa 1980
After his split with Art Garfunkel in 1970, Simon's solo career was well underway by the time this photograph was taken. Here, the singer appears as if he is the character from his song "Stranded in a Limousine," off the 1977 album *Greatest Hits, Etc.*

PRINCE
Terry Gydesen, 1993
Lisbon, Spain: Having recently become "the artist formerly known as," the Minneapolis-born star – whose birth name is Prince Rogers Nelson – was waiting in his limousine to go onstage when this photograph was snapped.

DR. DRE
Mark Seliger, 1993
Los Angeles: While on the site of a shoot for the former N.W.A member's video "Let Me Ride" – a song about a favorite car – Seliger took out a red handkerchief to wipe his forehead. He was warned to put it away at once – it had the wrong gang associations and could lead to trouble.

MICHAEL JACKSON
Barry Plummer, 1972
London: Fourteen-year-old Jackson was touring Europe when Plummer captured the then-exuberant singer. After spending the past three years with the Jackson 5, he released in 1972 his first solo album, *Got to Be There*, which yielded the Number One hit "Ben," about a pet rat.

BUDDY HOLLY
Lewis Allen, circa 1958
Rochester, New York: Allen caught Holly aboard the band bus. The other two passengers were probably members of a package show with whom Holly was touring. It was on such a tour, in 1959, that Holly was killed when he chose to fly rather than ride in the bus.

PETER GABRIEL
Anton Corbijn, 1986
Bath, England: Corbijn shot Gabriel near the musician's recording complex, Real World Studios. His breakthrough solo album, *So*, was released around this time, yielding the chart-topping "Sledgehammer." That same year, he joined the Amnesty International tour.

EMMYLOU HARRIS
David Gahr, 1975
New York City: Gahr first photographed Harris when she was a teenager performing in Greenwich Village folk clubs. This picture, taken in Central Park, coincided with the release of Harris's *Pieces of the Sky*, which took the singer to the top of the country charts. Gram Parsons had given Harris her C&W start by enlisting her to sing on his albums *G.P.* and *Grievous Angel*. Parsons died of an overdose in 1973, leaving Harris to keep his music alive.

CAPTAIN BEEFHEART
Anton Corbijn, 1980

From this Mojave Desert encounter, a deep friendship developed between Corbijn and Beefheart, a.k.a. Don Van Vliet, who later said: "I told him … just shoot the meat! … He brought out … my love of animals. He got parts of me I didn't even know I had. … Anton shoots the edges and occasionally … even the bent parts!"

VIV ALBERTINE
Anton Corbijn, 1980

Palm Springs, California: Corbijn had hopes of shooting the guitarist and her band, the Slits, in the buff for *Return of the Giant Slits*. (On their debut, *Cut*, the femme-punks wore only mud.) This day, however, the clothes stayed on.

VAN MORRISON
Elliott Landy, 1969

Woodstock, New York: Morrison was living in the town that gave the festival its name. Landy, also a village resident, took this photo in the backyard of the home of the Band's Richard Manuel and Garth Hudson. Other shots would grace the cover of 1970's *Moondance*.

ROBYN HITCHCOCK
Dan Borris, 1993

Around the time of Hitchcock's 1993 album, *Respect*, Borris framed the ex–Soft Boy leader striking a characteristically eccentric pose.

JACKSON BROWNE
Frank W. Ockenfels 3, 1993

Photographing Browne after the release of his tenth album *I'm Alive*, Ockenfels wanted to capture an "older and wiser" Browne without playing into the hype surrounding his recent breakup with actress Daryl Hannah.

CAROLE KING
Kurt Markus, 1992

Montana: On her ranch in Big Sky Country, the fifty-year-old King displayed "her charm and generosity and touchable womanliness," recalled Markus.

LEONARD COHEN
Raeanne Rubenstein, circa 1970
Nashville, Tennessee: For this photo session, Rubenstein traveled to the farm where Cohen lived. She found the idiosyncratic Canadian singer–songwriter, who had recently released his third album, *Songs of Love and Hate*, "handsome, friendly and naturally poetic."

STING
Kevin Westenberg, 1992

Wiltshire, England: This photo came from the cover shoot for *Ten Summoner's Tales* – Sting's fourth platinum LP. The ex-Police-man later told ROLLING STONE, "I don't feel guilty for being rich and famous."

ROGER DALTREY
Terry O'Neill, 1978
Sussex, England: O'Neill photographed the thirty-four-year-old singer at his country estate to show a different side from his onstage persona with the Who – the preeminent instrument-smashing band. *Who Are You* was released the same year; in September drummer Keith Moon died of a drug overdose.

THE ROLLING STONES
Arthur Elgort, 1981
Elgort joined the Stones at a Massachusetts farm where they were rehearsing for the *Tattoo You* tour. When Keith Richards unexpectedly climbed onto a horse, Elgort said he was delighted, because both the animal and the guitarist were "lazy and gray."

THE BAND
Elliott Landy, 1969

Woodstock, New York: Levon Helm, Robbie Robertson, Richard Manuel, Rick Danko and Garth Hudson had been rehearsing that summer in the living room of a house overlooking the Ashokan Reservoir. The Band didn't want to take too much time away from playing, so they did the session in the backyard. Some shots were used for the group's acclaimed second album, *The Band*.

BOB DYLAN
Elliott Landy, circa 1970

Woodstock, New York: Dylan invited his friend Landy over one day to help assemble a new trampoline. Landy then captured Dylan at play, on the trampoline and off.

TOM WAITS
Frank W. Ockenfels 3, 1992

Having just played the deranged Renfield in 1992's *Bram Stoker's Dracula*, Waits showed up with a carful of props to use for the session. Ockenfels finally asked him to pose for a straightforward head shot, which Waits could only tolerate for a few minutes. In this final frame, Waits was growling for Ockenfels to stop.

NATALIE MERCHANT
Jon Ragel, 1989

Detroit: Before a show at an outdoor auditorium on a very hot afternoon, Merchant and her band, 10,000 Maniacs, wandered onto a nearby golf course. The sprinklers happened to come on, and the sweaty, uncomfortable shoot was saved.

BILLY JOEL
Mary Ellen Mark, 1987

Red Square, Moscow: Mark photographed the thirty-eight-year-old Joel during his summer tour, which was being filmed by her husband. Joel was the first U.S. pop star to take a fully staged rock production to the Soviet Union. The album *Kohuept* documented the shows.

FRANK ZAPPA
David Gahr, 1967

New York City: Gahr, who frequently covered the Greenwich Village music scene in the sixties, photographed the twenty-seven-year-old Zappa the night he and the Mothers of Invention appeared at Cafe Au Go Go on MacDougal Street. The Grateful Dead played upstairs at the club on the same evening.

DAVID BOWIE
Terry O'Neill, 1974

London: During a shoot for the post–Ziggy Stardust LP *Diamond Dogs* (an adaption of Orwell's *1984*), the oversized canine "suddenly started to try and sing," O'Neill recounted, "much to mine and David's astonishment."

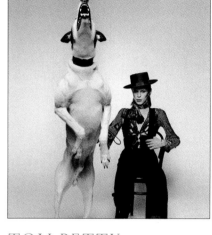

TOM PETTY
Mark Seliger, 1991

Joshua Tree National Monument, California: This photo session was set up to promote the album *Into the Great Wide Open*. "The camel actually ran away with me at one point," Petty reminisced bemusedly. "I'd say all in all a miserable day."

DWIGHT YOAKAM
Mark Seliger, 1993

Hollywood: It was decidedly not Nashville, so Seliger rented a horse for a photo session on Hollywood Boulevard. The chaps and stance, he said, were unmistakably Yoakam. The maverick country crooner had recently released his sixth album, *This Time*, and portrayed a trucker in the film *Red Rock West*.

VILLAGE PEOPLE
Bill King, 1979

King shot the original members – biker Glenn Hughes, construction guy David Hodo, Navy man Victor Willis, sailor Alex Briley, cowboy Randy Jones and Indian Felipe Rose – as they gained notoriety for their double-entendre songs "Y.M.C.A." and "Macho Man."

THE EAGLES
Henry Diltz, 1972
California: On a Western movie set, Diltz and the band were inspired by an old photo. In the re-creation, roadies, producers and a graphic artist made up the posse who killed the outlaws portrayed by *(from left)* Jackson Browne (with mustache), Eagles Bernie Leadon, Glenn Frey, Randy Meisner and Don Henley, and J.D. Souther.

WILLIE DIXON, BIG JOE WILLIAMS, MEMPHIS SLIM
David Gahr, 1961
New York City: Gahr encountered the trio – bassist-songwriter Dixon, forty-six; blues shouter Williams, fifty-eight; and pianist Memphis Slim, forty-six – as they emerged from a recording session for Folkways.

JANET JACKSON
Yuri Elizondo, 1993
This photo was taken at Long Beach Airport the same year that her fifth album, *janet.,* leapt to the top of the charts, as did the single and video for "That's the Way Love Goes." Jackson's image was becoming more overtly sexual: That fall she would appear bare-breasted on a ROLLING STONE cover.

THE BEASTIE BOYS
David LaChapelle, 1986
New York City: After the release of the Beasties' debut, *Licensed to Ill,* the rambunctious trio met LaChapelle in Midtown for this portrait. He had Adam "Ad-Rock" Horovitz, Adam "MCA" Yauch and Michael "Mike D" Diamond approach the camera and make the goofy faces that would become the group's trademark.

JOHN LYDON
Anton Corbijn, 1983
The Dutch photographer shot Lydon, once known as Johnny Rotten, in Hoboken, New Jersey, with the Manhattan skyline across the Hudson River. Lydon had recently moved to New York City and was promoting the film *Corrupt,* starring the ex-Sex Pistol and Harvey Keitel.

MICHAEL HUTCHENCE
Enrique Badulescu, 1990
Los Angeles: The thirty-year-old lead singer of INXS danced constantly throughout the session, which was done about the time the group released *X.* The Australian band had been together for ten years before hitting the pop stratosphere with the 1987 album *Kick.*

SIMON AND GARFUNKEL
Photographer unknown, circa 1965
New York City: Having first begun harmonizing together as sixth-graders in Queens, New York, Paul Simon and Art Garfunkel initially called their vocal duo Tom and Jerry. (MICHAEL OCHS ARCHIVES)

MICK JAGGER
Peter Anderson, 1981
London: At a press conference the Rolling Stones held in the backyard of Soho's Le Beate Route club, Anderson, "overwhelmed by the paparazzi and Jagger himself," snapped a picture and captured both.

GRAHAM NASH
Graham Nash, 1974
New York City: This self-portrait, which Nash entitled "Portrait in the Plaza," is one of many photographs the singer-songwriter has taken of himself and fellow musicians.

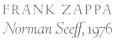

FRANK ZAPPA
Norman Seeff, 1976
Los Angeles: Seeff saw the thirty-six-year-old Zappa as a genius, someone who "would improvise with anything that was lying around and keep going, image after image."

LITTLE RICHARD
Photographer unknown, 1962

At the height of his success, the singer renounced rock & roll for gospel, becoming an ordained minister in the Seventh-Day Adventist Church. He did not, however, renounce his gleeful spirit.
(COLIN ESCOTT/SHOWTIME ARCHIVES, TORONTO)

FABIAN
Photographer unknown, 1959

Teen idol Fabian had just turned from singing to acting – his Top Ten hit "Hound Dog Man," an imitation of Elvis Presley, was also the title of his first film. The following year, he would costar with John Wayne in *North to Alaska.* (GLOBE PHOTOS)

AMES BROWN
Photographer unknown, 1967

In the midst of a rigorous year of touring and recording, including "Cold Sweat – Part 1," the Hardest Working Man in Show Business pauses for a recreational moment. Brown had been a semi-pro boxer as a teenager. (ARCHIVE PHOTOS)

MICK FLEETWOOD AND JOHN McVIE
Mark Seliger, 1992

Los Angeles: Seliger thought of the wedding-theme idea because the performers were – after having been together in Fleetwood Mac for twenty-five years – essentially married to one another. When Fleetwood heard the suggestion, he immediately declared that he should be the bride.

ARLO GUTHRIE
Mary Ellen Mark, 1969

Mark had met the singer-songwriter on the set of the movie *Alice's Restaurant,* based on Guthrie's 1967 recording. He invited her to his wedding to Jacklyn Hyde, where Mark took this snapshot – not even an official wedding portrait. That summer, Guthrie, the son of legendary folksinger Woody Guthrie, appeared at Woodstock.

COURTNEY LOVE
Guzman, 1992

Los Angeles: At home with Kurt Cobain and Frances Bean, Love was asked if she could be photographed undressed. She agreed, at ease with her postnatal body.

DION
Al Wertheimer, 1958

Bronx-born Dion DiMucci and his group, the Belmonts, had recently charted for the first time when Wertheimer photographed the teen crooner enjoying a big Italian meal at home with his mom. The next spring the group's smash "A Teenager in Love" hit Number Five. (MICHAEL OCHS ARCHIVES)

MOTHERS OF INVENTION
Art Kane, circa 1968

For this *Life* magazine session, Kane wanted to portray the musical group as a family and took the idea of mothers – and their babies – as a theme. He gathered some of the musicians' infants, then booked about thirty more from a modeling agency. As soon as they began to shoot, one of the babies urinated, which inspired the others to do so as well, creating, in Kane's words, "the fountains of Rome."

DONOVAN
Chris Walter, circa 1965

Born Donovan Leitch in Glasgow, Scotland, the folksinger's debut album, *Catch the Wind,* with its hit title track, had recently put the spotlight on Britain's answer to Bob Dylan. (PHOTOFEATURES)

GEORGE HARRISON
Jurgen Vollmer, 1961

Only seventeen years old when the fledgling Beatles played Hamburg, Germany, in 1960, Harrison was deported for being underage. After his birthday in February 1961, the group returned for another stint in the spring, when this photo was taken. (STAR FILE)

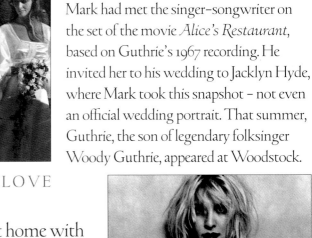

CHUCK BERRY
Jimmy Willis, 1957
Waco, Texas: The seminal rock & roller's song "School Day" had been a Number Three hit when this photo of Berry with his young fans was taken. His album *After School Sessions* was issued by Chess Records the next year.

(COLIN ESCOTT/SHOWTIME ARCHIVES, TORONTO)

NEIL YOUNG
Joel Bernstein, 1971
Sitting inside the small caretaker's cabin on his newly purchased Broken Arrow Ranch in northern California, the twenty-six-year-old Young took a break from writing the songs for 1972's *Harvest.* Bernstein believes the photograph expresses Young's "contemplative, interior mood."

THE GRATEFUL DEAD
Gene Anthony, circa 1967
San Francisco: Anthony took this portrait at the house at 710 Ashbury Street shared by the Dead – *(clockwise from front)* Ron "Pigpen" McKernan, Phil Lesh, Bob Weir, Bill Kreutzmann and Jerry Garcia.

BOB DYLAN
Elliott Landy, 1968
Woodstock, New York: Landy, having photographed Dylan for the *Saturday Evening Post,* visited the elusive songwriter, here holding his son Jesse, to show him the pictures – and had the opportunity to shoot some more.

JOHNNY CASH
Photographer unknown, circa 1960
After recording for Sun, Cash moved to Columbia in 1959. Here, on a rare respite from hard livin' on the road, he relaxes at home. (MICHAEL OCHS ARCHIVES)

ELVIS COSTELLO
Anton Corbijn, 1977
Amsterdam: Touring to promote his first album, *My Aim Is True,* the twenty-three-year-old Costello was crashing in a hotel room so small Corbijn had to squeeze his over-six-foot frame into a cupboard to get the shot.

LINDA RONSTADT
Annie Leibovitz, 1976
In the wake of *Heart Like a Wheel* and *Prisoner in Disguise,* which established Ronstadt as a major pop star, Leibovitz framed her in a domestic moment.

BRUCE SPRINGSTEEN
David Michael Kennedy, 1982
Brewster, New York: Springsteen used a Kennedy landscape photo for the cover of *Nebraska* and wanted him to take the publicity pictures as well. Kennedy exposed the singer-songwriter's then-solitary, inward nature, exemplified by the acoustic album that Springsteen recorded by himself on a four-track recorder.

BOB DYLAN AND JOAN BAEZ
Daniel Kramer, 1965
New Haven, Connecticut: After a concert, Kramer, Dylan, Baez and her family returned to the hotel and, several drinks later, went into a photographic frenzy. By 2:30 A.M., various props were involved, though Kramer doesn't remember how they got around to using the iron on Baez's hair.

ELVIS PRESLEY
Photographer unknown, 1957

To portray singer Deke Rivers in *Loving You*, Elvis dyed his hair black. The other young man here is thought to be his cousin Gene Smith. (JEFF CAHN COLLECTION)

PATTI SMITH
Robert Mapplethorpe, 1978

Becoming pals with Mapplethorpe in 1967, when he was an art student, Smith later said: "Robert helped me take all this totally nebulous energy and put it in a form."

MICK JAGGER
Terry O'Neill, 1963

O'Neill caught Jagger getting ready for an appearance on *Thank Your Lucky Stars*. The BBC-TV show's producer reportedly told the band's manager to replace "that vile-looking singer with the tire-tread lips."

SNOOP DOGGY DOGG
Jean Baptiste Mondino, 1994

Los Angeles: Mondino photographed Calvin Broadus the year he broke big: His Number One debut album, *Doggystyle*, became the biggest-selling rap album, and his song "Murder Was the Case" inspired a film of the same name directed by Dr. Dre.

BO DIDDLEY
Photographer unknown, circa 1958

The inventor of the rock & roll beat that bears his name, Bo Diddley, born in McComb, Mississippi, was photographed helping his bass player half-sister, the Duchess, with her do. (MICHAEL OCHS ARCHIVES)

ISAAC HAYES
Raeanne Rubenstein, circa 1980

Atlanta: Rubenstein arrived at Hayes's sparse plantation-style home as he was preparing for the session. She thought the soul singer's daily head-shaving ritual would make a better portrait than a more formal pose. Hayes agreed.

KATE BUSH
Anton Corbijn, 1981

London: Corbijn, who has said he strives "to show people as they really are," photographed the twenty-three-year-old Bush. When she was sixteen, Bush's four-octave voice caught the attention of Pink Floyd's David Gilmour, who guided her early career path.

BONNIE RAITT
Bill King, 1975

New York City: King shot the bottleneck slide guitarist and blues singer when her fifth album, *Home Plate*, came out. Although acclaimed, her mass popularity didn't arrive for fifteen years.

DAVID BYRNE
William Coupon, 1979

The twenty-seven-year-old Talking Heads mastermind, in his PJs, looks as if he'd just gotten the idea for the song "Stay Up Late," which would appear on the band's 1985 album, *Little Creatures*.

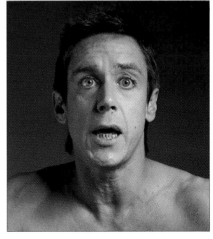

IGGY POP
Robert Mapplethorpe, 1981

Iggy once wrote, "I've been spit at, I've been slugged, I've been egged. I've been hit with paper clips, money, brassieres, underwear, old rags and expensive garments. . . . Yeah, you get used to it after a while."

GRACE JONES
Steven Klein, 1990

Paris, France: Born in Spanishtown, Jamaica, the six-foot-tall Jones transformed herself from model to cult-disco diva to rock-noir singer. Her first dance hit was 1977's "I Need a Man."

LaVERN BAKER
Photographer unknown, circa 1955

The R&B singing sensation was hitting her stride in the mid-fifties, though she got her start performing in the late forties.

(FRANK DRIGGS COLLECTION)

L.L. COOL J
Albert Watson, 1992

New York City: L.L. Cool J – for Ladies Love Cool James – had already recorded several rap classics, including "Going Back to Cali" and "Mama Said Knock You Out," when he posed for Watson.

CURTIS MAYFIELD
Mark Seliger, 1993

Mayfield was the architect of the sixties Chicago soul sound, as well as the man who wrote the theme for *Superfly*. Seliger met with the artist at his home outside Atlanta, Georgia. This shot, taken of Mayfield posed upright, depicts his continuing vibrance despite the complete paralysis resulting from a 1990 accident, when a lighting rig fell on him during an outdoor concert in Brooklyn, New York.

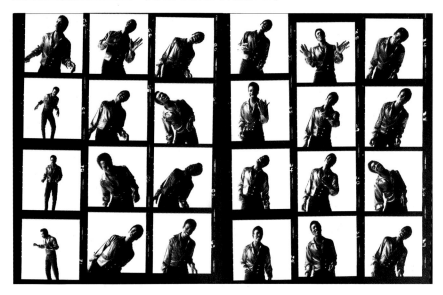

WILSON PICKETT
Jerry Schatzberg, 1967

New York City: During the photo session, Schatzberg played Pickett's records, including that year's smash "Funky Broadway," and the soul man cut loose, singing along while posing.

THE JEFFERSON AIRPLANE
Jim Marshall, 1967

San Francisco: For a *Look* magazine story, Marshall aimed his wide-angle lens at the two-year-old Airplane peering down upon him. The 1967 lineup included *(clockwise from bottom)* Marty Balin, Paul Kantner, Grace Slick, Jorma Kaukonen, Spencer Dryden and Jack Casady.

THE ROLLING STONES
Art Kane, circa 1969

London: Kane was granted only fifteen minutes to get a portrait of *(clockwise from top)* Bill Wyman, Brian Jones, Mick Jagger, Keith Richards and Charlie Watts. He did manage to catch the original lineup, though, for it soon changed: Jones left the band in June 1969 and died the next month.

GRACE SLICK; JERRY GARCIA
Herb Greene, 1966; 1967

San Francisco: The wall of hieroglyphics behind Slick and Garcia, in portraits taken a year apart, became a backdrop for many of the San Francisco performers Greene photographed in the late sixties. Though it came to be associated with the Matrix nightclub, it was actually the wall of Greene's dining room. He had steamed off the old wallpaper and found a beautiful patina underneath, with "Happy New Year" written across it. One day Greene's roommate drew the ancient symbols all over the wall, and, although Greene was furious at the time, the Egyptian imagery actually suited the psychedelic Haight-Ashbury scene perfectly.

MARVIN GAYE
Annie Leibovitz, 1972

Leibovitz's camera exposed a solitary, contemplative side of Motown's quintessential romantic. Gaye, then thirty-three, would be murdered by his father twelve years later.

NATALIE COLE
Peggy Sirota, 1993
Culver City, California: During the photo session at Smashbox Studios, Sirota played Cole's new album of standards, *Take a Look*, and the forty-three-year-old vocalist – the daughter of Nat King Cole – began to sing along.

KIM THAYIL; CHRIS CORNELL
Frank W. Ockenfels 3, 1993
Guitarist Thayil and front man Cornell of Seattle-based Soundgarden hated being photographed – their nine years of band experience hadn't helped. So Ockenfels placed his emphasis on the lighting by creating an effect like that made by the sun reflecting off the surface of a swimming pool.

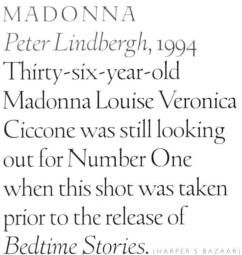

STEVEN TYLER
Dennis Keeley, 1989
Los Angeles: Photographing all five members of veteran rockers Aerosmith together that day was, according to Keeley, "a logistical nightmare"; the forty-one-year-old lead vocalist, however, "gave it his all – as usual," he said.

MADONNA
Peter Lindbergh, 1994
Thirty-six-year-old Madonna Louise Veronica Ciccone was still looking out for Number One when this shot was taken prior to the release of *Bedtime Stories*. (HARPER'S BAZAAR)

ICE-T
Mark Seliger, 1993
New York: Seliger used the duct-tape gag because the shoot occurred in the midst of controversy over "Cop Killer," by the rapper's rock band Body Count; the song was later removed from the group's LP.

NIRVANA
Mark Seliger, 1992
Seliger caught *(from left)* Dave Grohl, Kurt Cobain and Krist Novoselic after *Nevermind* had transformed the trio into reluctant superstars.

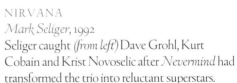

BOOTSY COLLINS
Dennis Keeley, 1988
Disappearing into the dressing room for three mysterious hours, the bass-playing funkmeister reemerged, Keeley reminisced, as "Moses from the mountain" – perfect in every detail, with twelve pairs of spectacles on hand.

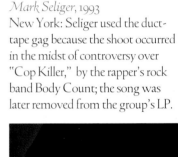

ACKNOWLEDGMENTS

This rock & roll tome would not have been possible without the contributions of numerous people. Many thanks to the distinguished photographers whose spectacular work graces these pages, as well as to ROLLING STONE's Jann S. Wenner, Kent Brownridge, John Lagana, Kevin Mullan, Tom Worley, Meera Kothari, Willis Caster, Christopher Popkie, Jodi Peckman, Sheryl Olson, Geraldine Hessler and Anthony Bozza. We are indebted to Little, Brown's Michael Pietsch, our heroic editor, and Clif Gaskill, our production czar, as well as our literary agent, Sarah Lazin – thank you for bringing this project to fruition!

Also much appreciated are the efforts of Laurie Kratochvil, Susan Richardson, Nancy Bilyeau, Will Rigby, Elizabeth Renaud, Kevin O'Dea, Sidney Painter, Carrie Smith, Catherine Wallace, Eric Siry, Yoomi Chong, Su-Mei Chan, Jeremy Fields, Marianne Burke, and Howard Musk and Joe Braff of Imago. We are grateful for the kindness of Jim Marshall, Michael Ochs, Jonathan Hyams, Helen K. Ashford, Virginia Lohle, Taki Wise, Bob Shatton, Kimberly Kriete, Alain Dister, Janet Ginsburg, Nathalie Vendeuge, Janet McClelland, Jeffrey Smith and Jeff Streeper.

Most of all, for their dedication and perseverance, kudos must go to Fred Woodward, Anthony DeCurtis, Denise Sfraga, Julie Claire Derscheid, Eric Flaum, Fredrik Sundwall and Greg Emmanuel.

And finally, of course, we'd like to express our admiration of and gratitude to the inspiring artists whose music – and images – capture rock & roll in all its timeless glory.

HOLLY GEORGE-WARREN, *Editor*
SHAWN DAHL, *Associate Editor*
Rolling Stone Press
March 1995

FRED WOODWARD joined ROLLING STONE as art director in 1987 and has also since been named creative director of Wenner Media. As a book designer, his most recent work is *Cobain*, published by Little, Brown and Company in 1994.

ANTHONY DeCURTIS is an editorial director at VH1 and a contributing editor to ROLLING STONE. He is the editor of *Present Tense: Rock & Roll and Culture* and coeditor of *The Rolling Stone Illustrated History of Rock & Roll* and *The Rolling Stone Album Guide*. He won a Grammy for his liner notes for the Eric Clapton retrospective *Crossroads* and has twice won ASCAP Deems Taylor Awards for excellence in writing about music. He holds a Ph.D. in American literature from Indiana University.